SHARPE, PALEY AND AUSTIN

Sharpe, Paley and Austin: A Lancaster Architectural Practice: 1836–1942

by
James Price

Centre for North-West Regional Studies
University of Lancaster
1998

For Kate:

an admirer of Paley and Austin from an early age

Sharpe, Paley and Austin: A Lancaster Architectural Practice: 1836–1942 by James Price

This volume is the 35th in a series published by the Centre for North-West Regional Studies at the University of Lancaster. Details of other titles in the series which are available may be found at the back of this volume.

Published by the Centre for North-West Regional Studies, University of Lancaster

Designed and typeset by Carnegie Publishing Ltd, Carnegie House, Chatsworth Road, Lancaster LA1 4SL

Printed and bound in the UK by Redwood Books, Wilts

British Library Cataloguing-in-Publication Data
A CIP catalogue record for this book is available from the British Library
ISBN 1–86220–054–8

Contents

Illustrations

Tables and graphs

Maps

Acknowledgements

We acknowledge with thanks permission to reproduce the following photographs:

No. 1 Lancaster Museum
No. 2 Mr Basil Austin
No. 6 The Grange Hotel
Nos 22–34 (inclusive) Geoffrey Sutcliffe
Nos 35–41 (inclusive) Lancashire Library
No. 50 Sedbergh School

Introduction

With the post-war revival of interest in Victorian architecture there has developed a new awareness of the role architects played in the development of the townscapes of nineteenth century Britain. At the same time researchers have become interested not only in the buildings themselves but with their creators too, in their training, their lives and in their status and role in society.

Studies exist now of most of the major national figures;[1] men like Pearson, Bodley, Street, Waterhouse, Lutyens and above all Scott.[2] Thus Howell and Sutton can say that 'The best known architects of the Victorian period are the great men with London offices, numerous assistants, pupils, and clerks of works and practices often extending over the whole of Britain'.[3] There has however been far less research into those other practices which had only a local or regional importance. Yet such 'general practitioner'[4] architects built up large practices and took on a wide variety of work including new churches, the restoration and alteration of existing churches, schools, public buildings, houses, factories and even railway commissions!

It is these men rather than the London based firms who left the greatest mark on the built environment of both town and country in Victorian times and provided a legacy that has come down to us. One such important provincial practice of the first rank was that run firstly by Edmund Sharpe, and later by E. G. Paley, H. J. Austin and H. A. Paley.

My own attention was first drawn to the work of this group of architects in the early 1970s. At that time I was running WEA classes in the Lancaster area and, in order to research material for my lectures and field excursions, spent a good deal of time in Lancaster Library. There I soon became aware of the many buildings that Sharpe, Paley and Austin had designed in and around Lancaster itself. During this same period my researches into the history of Congregationalism in Lancaster revealed that one such building was the High Street Sunday School designed by Paley in 1859. It was not however until somewhat later, when I had cause to visit Furness and Barrow, that I realised how much work Paley and later Paley and Austin had done in that area and how they were a practice of regional rather than local importance.

It therefore came as no great surprise to find that there were many people who shared my growing enthusiasm for the work of this practice. No one who has read the introductions to Sir Nicholas Pevsner's *North; and South Lancashire* (in the Buildings of England series) can be in any doubt as to the high opinion in which he held the three men 'this

1 Edmund Sharpe, 1809–1877.

2 Hubert James Austin, 1841–1915.

3 Edward Graham Paley, 1823–95.

Lancaster dynasty of architects did more work in the county, and for a time more outstanding work than any other'.[5] Others who have been or who are as interested as me both in the practice and the buildings they designed, include Robert Jolley, David McLaughlin, Colin Stansfield, Philip Browning, Gordon Smith, Bill Fuge, John Champness and the late Keith Ingham and T. W. Pennington. I owe a particular debt of gratitude to Robert Jolley, John Hughes and Bill Fuge for information on the partners and their work. Mr Basil Austin, grandson of H. J. Austin has also been of great assistance in helping to research the history of the Austin family.

In addition to our enthusiasm for this practice, we have all long shared the view that their work and its regional, indeed national, importance is insufficiently recognised today even with the revival of interest in Victorian architecture. In fact they have been neglected for too long by architectural historians and the general public. It was members of this group under the chairmanship of Andrew White of the Lancaster Museum, who were involved with Museum staff in the mounting of an Exhibition in Lancaster in 1994 (Paley and Austin: Lancaster Architects). A publication produced[6] (in the Lancaster Museum Local Studies series) in association with the exhibition incorporated a partial listing of their main works and some details of the partners themselves.

In 1991 as part of the reawakening of interest in the practice a Day School was held at the University of Lancaster organised by Dr Elizabeth Roberts of the Centre for North West Regional Studies on 'Sharpe, Paley and Austin'. This attracted a large, interested and knowledgeable audience, and four papers were presented, each by a person interested in one or more members of the practice. The whole day was very well received and it was suggested at its conclusion that it would be useful if either the papers themselves or a resume of them could be published and made available to a wider audience; something which is now being done.

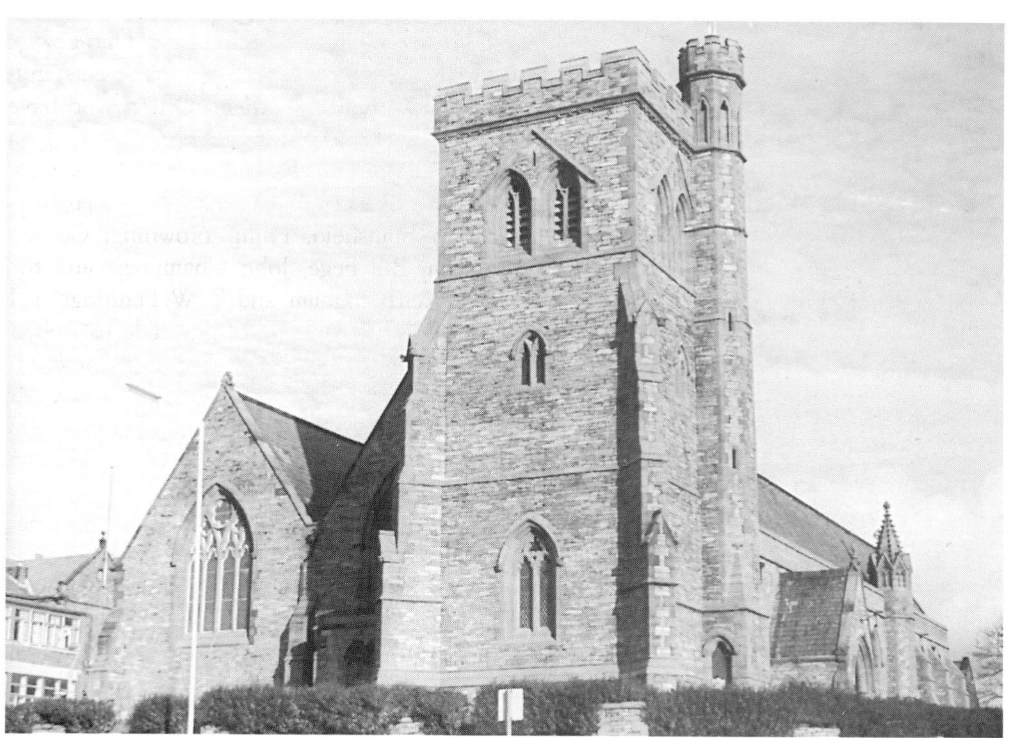

4 St George's Church, Barrow, 1859–61 by E. G. Paley.

Footnotes

1 J. Fawcett (ed.), *Seven Victorian Architects*, Thames and Hudson, 1976.
2 David Cole, *The Work of Gilbert Scott*, Architectural Press, 1980.
3 Peter Howell and Ian Sutton, *The Faber Guide to Victorian Churches* (in conjunction with the Victorian Society), Faber and Faber, 1989.
4 C. Brooks and A. Saint (eds), *The Victorian Church*, Manchester University Press, 1995.
5 N. Pevsner, *The Buildings of England: North Lancashire*, Penguin, 1969.
6 J. Price, *Paley and Austin. Architects of Lancaster*, Local Studies No. 19, Lancaster City Museums, 1994.

I

Sharpe, Paley and Austin: a historical outline of the firm, 1836–1944

The changing name of the firm

The beginnings of the architectural practice that was later to become Paley and Austin took place in 1836 when a young Cambridge graduate called Edmund Sharpe (1809–1877) set up as an architect in Sun Street, Lancaster. Two years later he took Edward Graham Paley (1823–1895) as a pupil, who upon completion of his articles became a partner in 1845. Now the practice had the first of a number of name changes (see Table 1) becoming Sharpe and Paley. By the late 1840s Sharpe was becoming less interested than he had been in architecture, passing over 'the bulk of the work' to Paley in 1847.[1] Finally in 1851 he retired, leaving Paley, now his brother-in-law , in charge of the practice.

From 1851 to 1868 Paley worked alone with John Douglas, a former pupil of Edmund Sharpe, as his chief assistant until either 1855 or 1860.[2] By 1867 the amount of work that the practice was obtaining, was obviously too much for one man and Paley set out to find a partner. In that year or early 1868 he was joined by Hubert James Austin (1841–1915) from the office of Sir George Gilbert Scott. Between 1867/8 and 1886 the two men worked together as Paley and Austin until they were joined by Paley's son Henry (Harry) Anderson Paley (1859–1946). The death of E. G. Paley in 1895 necessitated a name change to Austin and Paley, and a further change was necessary in 1914 when Austin's son Geoffrey (G. L.) joined the firm.

When H. J. Austin died in 1915 G. L. Austin was on active service and Harry Paley ran the practice and carried out what work was obtained during World War 1. At the end of the war however G. L. Austin did not return to the practice, there is an Austin family tradition that the practice could not support two partners,[3] and he left architecture for other fields. From 1918 until his retirement in 1936 Harry Paley carried on the practice alone though changing the name back to Austin and Paley around 1925, the name by which older Lancastrians still remember the firm.[4]

5 St John's Church, Hutton Roof, Cumbria, 1881–2 by Paley and Austin.

6 The Grange Hotel, Grange-over-Sands, 1866 by E. G. Paley.

Table 1:
Changes of name of the firm

1836–45	Edmund Sharpe, Architect
1845–51	Sharpe and Paley, Architects
1851–68	E. G. Paley
1868–86	Paley and Austin
1886–95	Paley, Austin and Paley
1895–1914	Austin and Paley
1914–1915	Austin, Paley and Austin
by 1925	Austin and Paley

At the outbreak of the Second World War, Austin and Paley is still recorded, as occupying the firm's offices at 24 Castle Park (though Paley had retired in 1936)[5] and some work was going on there until early in 1942. According to the City Rate Books, Austin and Paley last paid rates on their office in 1944. In that year the practice appears to have been wound up by Mr J. Tarney and the building used by the Home Guard. Eventually 24 Castle Park was sold to the City Council and later (after 1946) converted to flats.

The office staff

In a large and thriving practice like that of Paley and Austin there were a number of people employed other than the partners themselves. There would have been draughtsmen and clerical staff like J. E. Holden[6] (one of whom would have been in charge of the office), clerks of works and one or more 'pupils' attracted by the reputation of the architects who made up the practice, and who served their articles here. While we do not know the actual numbers of people in the office, it is unlikely to have been as large as the twenty seven who were in Gilbert Scott's office in 1856–61[7] but was certainly greater than the two or three that Norman Shaw had before 1876 (though he did have pupils who carried out many routine office tasks).[8]

An architect's training

During the lifetime of this practice there were only five partners, each of them a qualified

7 St George's Church, Stockport, 1893–7 by Paley, Austin and Paley.

8 Sedbergh School Chapel, built by the Brassingtons of Settle in 1897.

architect and all bar one (G. L. Austin) a member of the RIBA (The Royal Institute of British Architects). Only one of them had no architectural training. Edmund Sharpe had, upon completion of his travels in Europe, set up as an architect with little more background than the four to five days he spent with Rickman in 1832 copying from the latter's books and drawings (though on his travels he had made many sketches and written detailed descriptions of buildings.) This entry to architecture was unusual even then, and when Paley came to Lancaster in 1838 as a fifteen year old it was to do his articles with Sharpe. Hubert Austin was also articled, from 1860–64, to Tom Austin his elder half-brother in Newcastle. Upon completion of his articles he took the Voluntary Examination in 1864 to become an ARIBA. Obviously a fine prospect, he was in the office of Sir George Gilbert Scott between 1865 and 1867 and was the Pugin Student of 1866. Scott appears to have held him in high regard for in 1866 he allowed the building of a church at Ashford designed by Austin to go ahead, something he did not normally allow in the case of young men in his office. Harry Paley was articled to Paley and Austin at eighteen in 1877 but then sent to London to gain experience before returning to Lancaster in 1882.

Geoffrey Austin was trained by W. H. Brierley of York before returning to Lancaster and becoming a partner in the firm.

What form did the training of an architect take in the last century? This after all was the century which saw the development of the professions with new ones like architecture and engineering joining law and medicine. As early as 1834 the RIBA was set up and by the end of the century architects were seen as professionals with their own techniques and code of conduct. Training appears to become more formal and rigorous as the century develops but initially, as in the eighteenth century, it consisted of becoming either the apprentice or pupil of an architect[9] and being trained 'on the job' by him in his office. Such training, as Kaye has re-

9 St Mary's Church, Dalton, 1883–5 by Paley and Austin.

10 St Mary's Church, Widnes, 1908–10 by Austin and Paley.

marked,[10] could be haphazard and often inadequate. Pupillage, where the architect was paid a premium, began at seventeen in London (fourteen to sixteen in the Provinces) and lasted three to four years after 1871.

Saint[11] has described the work of Shaw's office under the control of his chief clerk Lethaby where, after the payment of a premium of £300, articles took three years. Firstly pupils were taught to measure up buildings and draw plans in the approved 'office style'. After two years they were sent to the Royal Academy lectures and often voluntarily attended the Architectural Association Class of Design. Next came the responsibility of coordinating the information on the job, entailing visiting clients, builders and the site. Finally a pupil would become the 'manager' for a commission, in some cases acting as the Clerk of Works.

During the time trainee architects spent in training they would be actively collaborating with their master on his commissions. In this way few buildings were completely the work of one man and within the designs of Sharpe could be the ideas and work of Paley, Tom Austin and Douglas.

It is likely that both E. G. Paley and H. J. Austin had a similar training to that given by Shaw to his pupils but, in the case of Paley, without the outside lectures. Most of the theory which they did not get in the office came from books. Later after 1882 there were the compulsory RIBA examinations to work for if one wished to become an Associate. This obviously required a more formalised type of training for articles, something undertaken later by Harry Paley and G. L. Austin.

There is definite evidence of a number of pupils who were articled to the practice for three or four years. Some have already been mentioned as they later became partners, but another interesting name to emerge is Tom

11 St Peter's Church, Field Broughton, 1893–4, by Paley and Austin.

12 St John the Baptist's Church, Pilling, 1885–7, by Paley and Austin.

Austin. Thomas (Tom) Austin was the son of the Rev. T. Austin and the elder half brother of H. J. Austin. We know that he was in Lancaster by 1839 because there are in existence (in London) a number of sketches of this date of Furness Abbey. Also Austin seems to have been a founder member and second Captain of the Lancaster Rowing Club in 1844.[12]

Along with E. G. Paley, Tom Austin was involved in collecting information for Sharpe's masterpiece, *The Architectural Parallels*, and amongst some drawings at RIBA are lithographs of Fountains Abbey and Rievaulx done by him and dated 1842–6.[13]

Tom may well have been the assistant to Sharpe in the rebuilding of his father's church at Redmarshall in 1845. He appears to have left Lancaster in the early 1850s and had his own practice in Newcastle by around 1854. One mystery is why did he not stay in Lancaster with Paley as his partner when Sharpe retired in 1851? Was there perhaps only enough work for one architect at this time? Another pupil who also became an architect in his own right is John Douglas. This well known and important Chester architect (1830–1911) was articled to Sharpe in the 1840s and after completing his articles stayed in Lancaster before leaving to set up his own practice in Chester. Richard Thomas Beckett, a nephew of Douglas, also spent some time in Lancaster, being articled to Paley in 1886 and leaving in 1890.[14] He then worked with Douglas until 1894 when he set up as an architect with Edward Rathbone in Liverpool.

There are probably others of this period we have yet to discover.[15] They include the following. 'R. W. Johnson ... formerly the pupil of E. G. Paley ... architect ... desires respectfully to call the attention of his friends and the public generally to his new address' (Liverpool 1881)[16] and Wilfred Ainslie son of the Rev Henry Ainslie of Windermere[17] in the 1870s.

One mystery is that of Bernard Austin (1873–1955). In his father's obituary he is recorded as having done his articles with Austin and Paley. Unfortunately the RIBA have no record of this, and it is possible that, rather than undertaking a long articleship, Bernard merely gained some experience with his father's firm before leaving Lancaster for Liverpool.

There are a number of other names which crop up with reference to the practice but many of them were probably never qualified as architects and had a variety of other jobs within the firm. Thus we have T. Baines, whose plans of Lancaster Priory are dated 1882 and who was still working as Clerk of Works for Thornton in Lonsdale Church in 1936; William Wright, described as a Quantity Surveyor in the work at Giggleswick School in 1886; Mr S. Wright, Mr J. Thompson and Mr J. B. Slinger and finally Mr J. Tarney, who though not a qualified architect ran the office after Mr Paley retired in 1936. All of these six men are listed in the obituaries of one or more of the partners as working for the firm. At the end of the life of the firm, Mr W. Slinger and Messrs Helm and Shadwell are remembered by Harold Jackson (of Thompson and Jackson, Lancaster). If the practice had survived the War and Tarney had not decided to finish some time between 1942 and 1944 could these latter young men have resurrected the practice? This is one question we cannot answer.

The site of the firm

13 St John the Baptist's Church, Flookburgh, 1897–1900 by Austin and Paley.

During the course of its life, where were the offices of the practice situated in Lancaster? Not surprisingly, just as the name underwent some changes so did the location of the office. In 1838 Sharpe was listed as living in Sun Street and in the absence of a separate address for his office it was probably there too. By 1841 with a growing practice and several pupils, he had moved to an address in St Leonardgate. The following year, one year before his marriage in 1843, he had a private address at 11 Fenton Street but had retained the offices of his practice in St Leonardgate (Number 34?) where they remained until 1859–60.[18] These offices stood at the corner of Phoenix Street and St Leonardgate, where later the first Centenary Church was built, and afterwards replaced by the Drill Hall.

In 1859–60 E. G. Paley moved the firm's offices onto Castle Hill. This was a much smarter part of town and a more prestigious address, better suited to the growing practice of this now well known architect. This is where the offices were to stay until 1944. It is possible that they remained in the same building for the whole time, but it is difficult

14 St James' Church, Poolstock, Wigan, 1866 by E. G. Paley.

to be sure that in the early days they did not move within Castle Park. The conveyance between William Dunn and E. G. Paley on what is now 24 Castle Park is dated 1871, but Paley did not obtain a mortgage on the property until 1881.[19] In 1886 the office number is recorded as 31 Castle Park but in 1913 it is recorded as 24. Perhaps this could be the result of re-numbering. Today number 24 is a tangible reminder of the firm standing next to the Storey Institute facing the Castle Gate. It was built as a private house in c1767 and owned by Dr Wright until 1797. According to Cross Fleury[20] it was later for a time used as the Town Clerk's Office and eventually it became the home of the firm. At some time after its erection a small building with a large north facing window was added to the east end. This, it used to be thought, was built by Paley and Austin as a drawing office, but recent research shows that this addition was never used by the firm.

In addition to their Lancaster office, Paley and Austin also, for a time, had an office in Barrow-in-Furness. This rapidly growing industrial town, together with the other towns and villages of Furness, provided the firm with a large number of commissions, including those for the Furness Railway. It was obviously an advantage to have an office in the centre of the area which was providing so much work, and it is yet another piece of evidence of the growth and importance of the firm. Paley had done some work in this area before he was joined by Austin, but the first recorded date for the office at 16 Church Street is in the 1875 Town Directory. By 1896 however the practice address is given as Lancaster, and the Barrow office had disappeared; Stansfield suggests that it closed in 1890.[21] Thus for around twenty years Paley and Austin had a presence in a town and area other than Lancaster.[22] Though they closed their Barrow office, they continued to do work there including the North Lonsdale Hospital and St Mary's, Walney in 1907–8.

The effect of the firm on Lancaster's economy

Finally there is the question of what was the overall impact of the firm and its activities upon the economy of the town. This is the area of concern which holds out the most promise for further work. It is becoming more obvious all of the time that besides the large staff they were employing in their offices, their work in designing buildings which then had to be erected, had considerable implications for other local firms in terms of contracts and the subsequent employment of their workforces. In studying the details of the erection and embellishment of their buildings, one rapidly becomes aware of the role Lancaster firms played in all of the building trades. There is the frequent repetition of the name of James Hatch and Sons in relation to woodworking (they had an ecclesiastical woodworking shop in Penny St), and in addition were involved in erecting buildings.

15 St James' Church, Barrow, 1867–9 by E. G. Paley but the spire must be by H. J. Austin.

Other firms mentioned are Gillow and Co.; Charles Blades; G. Wright; A. O. Thoms (Stonemasons); Cross's (Slaters); Sewards (Heating and Plumbing); Thompson and Jackson and Shrigley and Hunt (stained glass and other work, e.g. an alabaster reredos). In the building of Ripley Chapel in 1889 the following firms 'all of Lancaster' are detailed.[23] Stonework ... W. Warbrick; Carpentry and Joinery ... C. Blades; Plumbing, Glazing, Gas Fitting and Heating ... A. Seward and Co.; Wood and Stone Carving ... H. T. Miles and Co.

The largest of these local firms was James Hatch and Sons, founded in 1844 and having by 1889 over one hundred hands employed in woodworking and contracting with large premises of over one acre in extent at the top of King Street. A Directory of 1889 describes them as 'being chiefly engaged in large contract works and ... undoubtedly among the most extensive concerns in their line in England. They make a leading and predominant speciality of church work of the most artistic class ... and they have clients in all quarters of the United Kingdom'.[24]

From firms like Hatch's went superb pieces of woodwork both for Paley and Austin churches and for their other buildings. In addition they carried out commissions for individual items of ornamental woodwork like pulpits, altars and reredoses designed by Paley and Austin for other architects' churches.

As well as using Lancaster firms they also made constant use of small local firms in areas where they had a number of contracts. Thus Henry Brassington of Settle carried out nine contracts for the firm between 1889 and 1936, including Sedbergh School Chapel in 1895.[25]

In some areas of work Paley and Austin made use of Lancaster firms to undertake commissions at a distance from home. Thus Lancaster masons and other tradesmen worked on contracts away from Lancaster during the week and returned home at the weekends. The tracery for Hertford Parish Church was carved in Lancaster and then sent by rail to Hertford. This sort of action and the evidence that masons particularly worked on contracts at a distance from Lancaster may help to explain, in part, why the firm's churches are so distinctive and the stonework of such quality. Did the masons, especially those doing the intricate carving, and particularly the foreman masons themselves, often come from Lancaster? If this is the case, it makes the involvement of Paley and Austin with the Lancaster building firms even more significant than just stimulating local development; they also had a regional influence on the erection and building of churches.

Footnotes

1 Edward Hubbard, *The Work of John Douglas*, The Victorian Society, 1991.

2 Ibid., p. 27.

3 E.g. 'the Great War sapped the economic foundations of major church building.' Brooks and Saint, *op cit.*

4 The Specification Book of Austin and Paley 1925–39, in the County Record Office (DDSr 10/1) gives the firm's name as Austin and Paley from 1925.

5 Interview with Mr Brassington (in November 1992), though *The Builder*, 31 May 1946, says he continued in active practice until 1939.

6 Recorded as Clerk to Messrs Paley and Austin when he became a member of the Lancaster Cricket Club in 1880. J. J. Gilchrist, *The Lancaster Cricket Club 1841–1909*. Lancaster, 1920.

7 David Cole, *The Work of Gilbert Scott*, The Architectural Press, 1980, p. 86. He quotes from the memoirs of T. G. Jackson who was a pupil in Scott's office 1858–61 and included pupils, assistants and clerks.

8 Andrew Saint, *Richard Norman Shaw*, Yale University Press, 1983.

9 An apprentice paid for his training by his services, but a pupil paid a premium and received no salary. Pupillage became increasingly popular as the century developed with the middle classes who could afford the premium.

10 B. Kaye, *Development of the Architectural Profession in Britain*, Allen and Unwin, 1960.

11 Saint, *op cit.*

12 N. Wigglesworth, *A History of Rowing in Lancaster*, Lancaster Museum Local Studies no. 17, 1992, p. 26. In 1845 the winning crew of the Lancaster Regatta Borough Cup consisted of Stroke – R. Atkinson; Number 3 oar W. Whelan; Number 2 oar T. Austin; Number 1 oar E. G. Paley.

13 RIBA Drawings Collection London, Y10. Drawings for *The Architectural Parallels*.

14 Letter from the Rev D. G. F. Hinge, 1989.

15 Who were M. Fielding and R. J. Withers whose names also appear on drawings for *The Architectural Parallels*? Were they pupils in the office of Edmund Sharpe?

16 Personal communication from C. Stansfield.

17 He became a member of the Lancaster Cricket Club in 1878. Gilchrist *op cit.*

18 In 1852 there is mention in the *Lancaster Guardian* of Messrs. Sharpe and Paley having a Counting House and show rooms on Parliament Street,

19 Information obtained by Dr Andrew White from the Council Deeds.

20 Cross Fleury, *Time Honoured Lancaster. Historic notes on the Ancient Borough of Lancaster*. Lancaster, no date.

21 The last Directory entry is in Slater's *Directories* of 1890.

22 In the *Barrow News* of 7 April 1896 there is an obituary of a Mr Harrison who for over twenty-five years had been the local representative of Paley and Austin (information from Peter Robinson).

23 Information from Ethel Geddes of the Lancaster Reference Library.

24 *Lancaster a Century Ago*. Introduction by James Price, Landy Press, 1990. Originally published as part of a Directory of Lancaster by the Historical Publishing Company in 1889.

25 Interview with Mr J. Brassington, *op. cit.*

2
Lancaster: a brief economic and social background

By 1836 when Sharpe began his architect's business, the fortunes of Lancaster had begun to improve with an increase in coastal trade using the port, and the development of the canalside mills. This improvement was in contrast to the period after 1815 when the international trade of the port had collapsed and commercial confidence was shattered by the collapse of the town's two banks in 1822 and 1826.[1] The population in 1836 was c.13000 (see Table II), an increase of some 20 per cent since 1821. However this growth was not to be sustained, and the period 1831–1861 saw little growth in the population of the town. It is the period 1861–1901 which saw the greatest growth both in the population and spatial extent of the town. While 1861–71 had a growth of 18.6 per cent over the previous ten years this was the smallest increase which takes place in the next thirty years. The final forty years of the nineteenth century saw Lancaster develop as an industrial town, a function to add to its existing market and service functions. The fact that 1901–1911 only saw an increase of 2.6 per cent is evidence that the town's growth was over.

16 St Peter's Church, Westleigh, 1880–1 by Paley and Austin.

The decline of the port after 1815 was the result of the extinction of the former transatlantic trade and the associated, port-related industry. Of this industry the only part to continue was the manufacture of furniture and cabinet making using imported woods, by Gillows and other smaller firms. Trade was never to return to the St George's Quay, but there was the growth of the grain and timber trade at Glasson together with the shipment of coal along the canal for the Lancaster mills which developed in the main after 1820.[2]

By the time Edmund Sharpe put up his plate in Fenton Street, Lancaster was chiefly a market and service centre for a wide rural area of North Lancashire and West Yorkshire. It was also a route centre, especially for traffic to and from Scotland and Yorkshire, and was well endowed with hotels and inns. The opening of the Lancaster and Preston Junction Railway in 1840 and the (Little) North Western in 1849 further stimulated the development of the town as a route centre.

17, 18. St Silas' Church, Blackburn. The church is by Paley and Austin 1894–8 and the tower, a later addition, is 1913–14 by Austin and Paley.

Table II
*Population of Lancaster, 1861–1911**

Year	population	Intercensal increase (%)
1801	9,030	
1811	9,247	2.42
1821	10,144	9.4
1834	12,613	20.6
1841	13,531	9.1
1851	14,738	5.0
1861	14,487	0.9
1871	17,245	18.6
1881	20,663	28.8
1891	33,254	29.8
1901	40,329	20.6
1911	41,410	2.6

Intercensal figures provided by A. G. Boulton
*(Lancaster Borough & Skerton, Scotforth, Bulk, Aldcliffe)

Unfortunately just as the transport role was developing, another function, that of legal centre, was in decline. Until 1835 one of the features of the life of the town had been the twice yearly Assizes. To these had flocked wealthy and polite society, with some gentry having houses in the town for this purpose. To these must be added the lawyers and judges, and the whole produced a 'season' marked by balls and other social activities. In 1835 the Assizes to South Lancashire were removed to Liverpool and from now on the Lancaster ones were a pale imitation of their former glory and Lancaster's reputation as a fashionable resort for the gentry fell into rapid decline.

From 1840 to the end of the century Lancaster slowly but surely developed into an industrial town. This industrial growth was not in cotton alone, as in so many other Lancashire towns, but in a more widely based group of industries. The development of carriage and waggon building followed the arrival of the railways in the town, and firstly the Dunn and later the Phoenix Factory were

19 St Stephen's Church on the Cliffs, Blackpool, 1924–6, by H. A. Paley.

20 St Matthew's and St James' Church, Mossley, Liverpool, 1870–5, by Paley and Austin.

involved in this activity, to be followed by the Lancaster Waggon and Carriage works in 1863. It was the inception and growth of the two firms – James Williamson and Sons from 1844 and William and Thomas Storey after 1848 – which really developed the town. These two family firms took over the majority of the canalside mills to make grey cloth which they used in the manufacture of floor and table coverings. Later with the development of their works on the riverside Williamson's added the manufacture of linoleum after 1887. These two firms, together with Gillow's and the railway related industry, were to provide the bulk of employment in the town by 1900. In 1911 30 per cent of both men and women in Lancaster were involved in the manufacture of floor coverings, linoleum and oil cloth. Now the town was an important industrial centre, a role it retained until the savage period of de-industrialisation in the 1960s and 1970s.

As the town grew, so did its service role. By the end of the century Lancaster was the provider of a range of medical and social services for a large part of the county. In addition to the Royal Lancaster Infirmary of 1896 (the successor of a smaller earlier hospital in Thurnham Street) it had the County Lunatic Asylum on the Moor (begun in 1812–16) and the Royal Albert Hospital built 1867–1873 (see Table III). There were two orphanages too (Ripley Hospital and Nazareth House). The development of all of these provided work for the practice, especially the Royal Albert and the enormous extensions at the Moor, as well as schools and a range of public buildings.[3]

Table III
Inmates and staff of the Moor,
the Royal Albert Hospitals and Ripley Orphanage

Lunatic Asylum	(1911)	2327 inmates	268 officials and families
Royal Albert	(1911)	679	110 officials
Ripley Orphanage	(1900)	330 children	—

By 1914, when the First World War broke out, the town had become very different from that in which the practice had first started. Not only was it larger, more populous and with a strong industrial base, but now the Liberal manufacturing and retailing classes ran the town.

Instead of being a one man band as in 1836, the practice was now a large one with a national reputation and which had just come second in the competition for the Liverpool Cathedral.

The Role of the Partners in Lancaster Society

As the biographies will reveal, each of the four men who ran the practice up to 1914 were fully involved in both the professional and the social life of Lancaster. Of these four, Sharpe with his political as well as cultural activities, was the most heavily involved outside of architecture, though Paley too, had a brief political career and was certainly perceived as being an important member of Lancaster society. Austin was, of these three, the least interested in public life, which he appears largely to have shunned in favour of family life, including music and painting. At the same time he was heavily involved in the life of the Priory Church which remains today largely a monument to his work.

By the time Harry Paley entered Lancaster society in the 1880s, the town was a very different place to that which his father would have known forty years before, or Sharpe for that matter in 1836. Lancaster had changed from being a commercial and service centre into an industrial town. Now a small but extremely wealthy group of local entrepreneurs had replaced the merchants, local gentry (and small professional class) as the local 'social and political elite'.[4] That the profession of architecture still meant something in society, however, is shown by the invitation of Lord Ashton to Henry Paley to shoot over the Ashton Estate in 1897.

The three earlier men were very much a part of the small professional and educational elite of the town at a time when Lancaster had no institution of higher education. As such they were not only seen as professional men through their training and education, but as equals and persons of consequence, by the society of the town.

Until the 1860s, as Winstanley has demonstrated, Lancaster contained a much higher percentage of professional men than almost any other Lancashire town.[5] These were men who were mainly lawyers, doctors, chemists, architects[6] and grammar school masters. Table IV is taken from directories for the period and shows the small numbers in this high status group. It was men like these and their families, plus the local gentry and the remaining merchants in the town, who were involved in the sporting, cultural and intellectual life of Lancaster.

In the early years of the century societies like the Choral Society; the Literary, Scientific and Natural History Society; the Literary and Philosophical Society, as well as the cricket, rowing, and archery clubs, were chiefly frequented by middle class families. Later this list was greatly extended by a range of sporting clubs, Football, Rugby Union, Swimming and an additional Rowing Club (John o'Gaunt). More artistic and cultural interests were catered for with the foundation of a Field Naturalists' Club, Amateur Dra-

21 Holker Hall 1873. The new wing added by Paley and Austin.

matic and Operatic Society, Orchestral Society and a Photographic Society.

Any analysis of the membership and attendance at functions of these and other societies continues to throw up the same names. Thus Sharpe was involved in the foundation of the Choral Society and both Mrs Austin and her mother were heavily

22 St Peter's Church (now Cathedral), Lancaster, 1857–9 by E. G. Paley. (Geoffrey Sutcliffe)

involved in this. Austin was a keen amateur musician and played in local orchestras. Paley was a founder of the British Archaeological Society and involved in the Mechanics Institute. This had been founded in 1824 and by 1856 it occupied a large house on the corner of Meeting House Lane and Castle Hill. It was to be rebuilt between 1887 and 1891 at the expense of Thomas Storey and to the designs of Paley and Austin. He was then a member of the Storey Institute Committee and took a 'warm and deep interest in Art Education in Lancaster' and was Secretary of the Art School until his death. In addition he was a Fellow of the Royal Institute of British Architects, and Committee Member and Examiner. In the last quarter of the century the growth in population of the town saw increased numbers of salaried professionals and members of the retail and business community. These teachers, dentists, accountants plus the officers of the King's Own Regimental Depot at Bowerham helped to swell the numbers of the various societies.

One of the ways of entering this society was by marriage or family connection. Sharpe had an entry to it through his connections with the Satterthwaite family and the friendship of William Whewell. Later the fact that Paley became part of the Sharpe family by marrying Edmund's sister must have eased his entry, and this is also true of Austin who married Edmund's niece. In 1873 the marriage between Edmund Sharpe Junior and Alice Storey (daughter of William Storey, a partner in Storey Brothers) guaranteed that the partners in the practice had links with the new industrial elite that was to be increasingly influential in the life of the town by the end of the century.

Footnotes

1 Worstwick, Sons and Co., 1822; Dilworth, Arthington and Birkett, 1826.

2 J. W. A. Price, *Industrial Archaeology of the Lune Valley*, CNWRS, University of Lancaster, 1983.

3 Moor Hospital; Royal Albert Hospital; Nazareth House; RLI; Ripley Hospital and Chapel.

4 M. Winstanley, 'The Town Transformed', in *A History of Lancaster*, ed. A. White, Ryburn Press, 1993.

5 Winstanley, *op cit.*

6 'The profession of architect was still fairly select, there were probably not more than 500 in the whole country ... (in 1850) an elite of 228 constituted the Institute of British Architects'. Sir John Summerson, *Victorian Britain*, ed. Boris Ford, Cambridge, 1992.

23 Lancaster Royal Grammar School. The first building and Headmaster's House, 1851–2, by Sharpe and Paley. (Geoffrey Sutcliffe)

3
The Partners

Edmund Sharpe

Edmund Sharpe (1809–77) was born in Knutsford, Cheshire, the only son of Francis and Martha Sharpe. His father was the organist at the parish church and a music teacher to many of the children of the local gentry. Martha Whittaker, his wife, had a sister Mary living in Knutsford, who was the wife of Dr Peter Holland. It was through becoming part of the extended 'Holland Clan' that the family became involved with local society. As a child Edmund played with Elizabeth Stevenson, the future Mrs Gaskell, a niece too of Dr Holland. It is recorded that when, aged five, little Edmund was being drawn around in a nice little carriage with Elizabeth it overturned, leading to him breaking his arm.[1]

In 1824 after the death of his father (1823) his mother and sister left Knutsford to live in Lancaster near another sister, Esther, who was married to Benjamin Satterthwaite, wine merchant. After Sedbergh School, Edmund entered St John's College, Cambridge in 1829 and here came under the influence of Dr William Whewell, Fellow (later Master) of Trinity College, a friend of the Satterthwaites and someone he had earlier met on school holidays in Lancaster. Whewell had been interested since 1822 in architecture and was in 1835 to publish *Architectural notes on German churches with additional notes on Normandy and Picardy*.[2] It was Whewell who suggested to Edmund that he apply in 1832 for one of two University travelling Bachelorships (or scholarships) and that he should study the development of Romanesque and Gothic architecture in France and Germany.

It was upon Sharpe's return to England in 1836 that he decided to become an architect. Between 1836 and his 'retirement' from architecture in 1851 he designed over forty buildings,[3] both churches and secular commissions, with a final design at St Paul's Church, Scotforth in 1874. For his early churches he made use of Romanesque designs, a style he returned to for Scotforth at the end of his life. The rest of his churches were in the Gothic style, initially Early English style and later the Decorated, upon which he was to become the 'leading authority', through his researches and writings. As an architect he is perhaps best remembered for his 'Pot Churches'.[4] The first of these, St Stephen's Church, Lever Bridge, Bolton (1842) is unique 'in being the first English building of the nineteenth century to be constructed largely of terra cotta'.[5] It was followed by the Holy Trinity, Platt, Manchester in 1845 and St Paul's Church, Scotforth in 1874. In all three cases use was made of terra cotta both for constructional and decorative purposes though stone was also used for some of the walls.

In 1851 he transferred the chief charge of his practice to E. G. Paley, and thereafter pursued other interests, spending the years 1856–1867 outside Lancaster, chiefly in Wales, being particularly involved in railway work.

Sharpe, as befitted a graduate of the University of Cambridge, was a man of many talents and interests. These were academic, political, and were also concerned with sanitary reform, railways and industry. In addition he was a fine musician and sportsman. Given the small size and provincial nature of Lancaster it is perhaps not too fanciful to suggest that he was the nearest thing the town had to a 'Renaissance man'

24 Lancaster and Skerton Cooperative Society, New Street, Lancaster *c.* 1901 by Austin and Paley. (Geoffrey Sutcliffe)

in the middle of the last century. In 1848[6] he commenced the publication of the *Architectural Parallels* on the progress of architectural style in the twelfth and thirteenth centuries. He followed it in 1849 by a study of *Decorated Windows* and in 1851 published in *The Seven Periods of English Architecture*, his own classification of medieval architectural styles. He published a number of other books and articles, was considered the greatest authority on Cistercian Abbeys in England, and in 1875 was presented with the Gold Medal of the RIBA for his architectural writings. A keen 'field worker', he ran annual excursions for the Architectural Association in the early 1870s in various parts of the country and in 1874 'chaperoned' the society through the North of France. He died in 1877 in Milan where he was in process of collecting materials on the ancient churches of north Italy.

Table IV
Changes in Lancaster society, 1824–1881

	1824 (*Baines*)	1834 (*Pigot*)	1848 (*Slater*)	1851 (*Mannex*)	1881 (*Mannex*)
1 Law	24 attorneys	34	27 (inc. 1 barrister)	28 (inc. 1 barrister)	Solicitors 21
2 Dentists	0	0	0	1	5
3 Medicine	Doctors 4 Surgeons 10	Doctors 2 Surgeons 14	Doctors 4 Surgeons 10	Doctors 4 Surgeons 13	18
4 Chemists/ Druggists	4	6	9	10	8
5 Clergy	11	7	10	18	23
6 Teachers	18	19 (+ 6 professors)	23	25 (+ 4 professors)	53 (+1 professor)
7* Vets	2	0	0	4	1
8 Architects/	0	0	1	3	6
Land Surveyors	3	4	4	0	0
9 Accountants	2	2	3	5	9
10* Army Officers	0	1	0	0	14 (Militia)
TOTAL	78	95	91	111	149
Minus rows 7 & 10	76	94	91	07	134

Footnote sources

1824 E. Baines, *History, Directory and Gazetter of the County Palatine of Lancaster*, 1824, reprinted 1968, David and Charles.

1834 *National Commercial Directory for the Seven Northern Counties of England*, 1834, Pigot and Co., London and Manchester.

1848 *Royal, National and Commercial Directory of Lancashire and the manufacturing districts around Manchester*, I. Slater, Manchester.

1851 *History, Topography and Directory of Westmorland with Lonsdale and Amounderness in Lancashire*, Mannex and Co., 1851, reprinted by Michael Moon, 1978.

1881 *Topography and Directory of Lancaster*, P. Mannex and Co., 1881.

In 1841 he was elected to the Town Council, was made Mayor in 1848 and involved in political life until 1853. During this time he was the leader in the struggle for sanitary reform in the town and produced plans for new sewerage and water supply systems. The latter were the basis for the improved water system in the town after 1852, so that by 1855 Lancaster had a clean and plentiful water supply to replace its previously often contaminated supplies which were drawn from wells.

His involvement in railways seems to have started with his contribution to the Lancaster

25 Holy Trinity Church, Morecambe 1840–1, by Edmund Sharpe. (Geoffrey Sutcliffe)

and Preston Junction Railway, where he subcontracted for masonry work at the Lancaster end of the line. Later he was involved with the 'Little' North Western line to Morecambe and was Secretary and Traffic Manager for a time. In 1856 he left Lancaster due to his involvement on the Conway-Llanwrst Railway as engineer. Living abroad from 1863 to

1866, he was involved in a scheme to replace the horse drawn tram system of Geneva, and later with a railway line from Perpignan to Prades. Upon his return to Lancaster in 1867 he took up the running of the Phoenix Foundry, which he had owned since 1852 and which for a time had built and repaired railway rolling stock.

He was also involved in the cultural, social and sporting life of Lancaster. He was a fine musician, playing the organ and clarinet and a founder member of the Choral Society.[7] In addition to writing hymns he built a number of small harmoniums to accompany them. In 1843 he purchased the Theatre Royal, which had declined considerably with the contraction of the Assize 'season', and opened it as The Music Hall. This was used for concerts, lectures, and religious meetings, and in 1848 the Athenaeum was founded there. He sold the theatre to the Athenaeum Company in 1859, the Company Secretary of which was E. G. Paley.

In 1841 Sharpe was one of a number of local gentlemen who founded a Cricket Club in Lancaster. When a year later the Club was dissolved and a 'rowing club formed on the spot'[8] Sharpe was once again at the fore. A fine oarsman, he achieved a number of successes with a crew that included Tom Austin and Edward Paley.[9] With the revival of cricket after 1848 Sharpe appears frequently in the newspaper leading 'his team out to many notable and frequent victories'. He was in fact still playing when over sixty years of age and was a first class batsman.[10] He was always interested in new inventions, and it is recorded, that, on his return to Lancaster from France in 1869, he brought with him the first bicycle seen in the town!

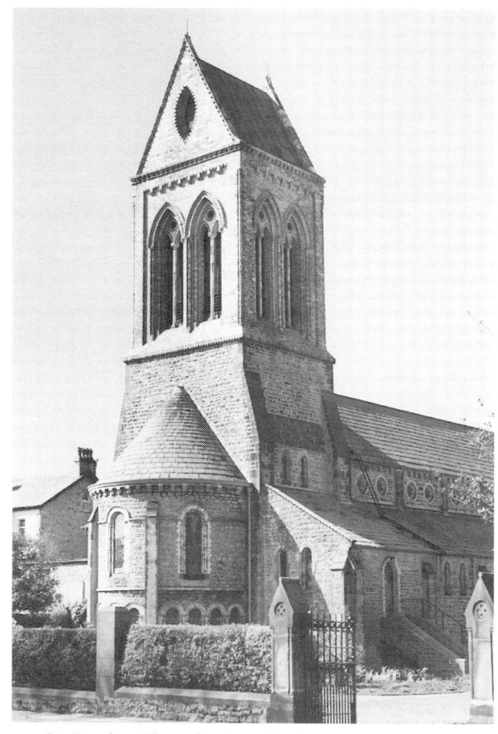

26 St Paul's Church, Scotforth 1874–6 by Edmund Sharpe. (Geoffrey Sutcliffe)

E. G. Paley

Edward Graham Paley (1823–95) was born at Easington near York in 1823, the fourth son of the vicar, the Rev Edmund Paley. He was the grandson of the eighteenth century divine, Archdeacon Paley, of whom it was said that it was always a source of surprise that he was never offered a bishopric. This, it was felt at the time, was because he had offended the King or Pitt, the Prime Minister. In fact it is more likely to have been due to his religious views.[11] His book *A View of the Evidences of Christianity* (1794) in which he gave a number of reasons for a belief in God was an attempt to defend the Christian faith from critics and sceptics, like Hume and Gibbon.

Edward Paley was educated at Christ's Hospital, London and while there was presented to the Duke of Wellington who gave him a gold guinea. In October 1838 he came to Lancaster as a pupil of Edmund Sharpe, and on the completion of his articles he was taken into the practice. Why he chose to be articled in Lancaster rather than elsewhere remains a mystery, but it may be because the Paley family was long established in the Settle area (the Archdeacon's father being the Headmaster of Giggleswick School for fifty four years), and thus knew Lancaster. The fact that his elder brother, Frederick Apthorpe[12] Paley, while not a strict contemporary of Sharpe had also been at St John's College may also have something to do with it, while his cousin Thomas was a contemporary of Sharpe at both Sedbergh and St John's College.[13] It would certainly appear that Edward's training in architecture led Frederick to become interested in church building, something which resulted in his *Manual of Gothic Buildings* in 1845.[14]

From 1851, when Sharpe 'retired', Paley worked alone, with pupils and assistants, until the arrival of Hubert Austin in 1868. During this time he designed a large number of buildings ranging from churches to private houses, public buildings to industrial and railway premises. In his obituary it says that 'in ecclesiastical architecture, probably no other architect ... has for so long a period occupied the prominent position enjoyed by Mr Paley in regard to Church architecture'. However it has to be said that while a sound architect, Paley never surpassed his achievement in designing St Peter's Cathedral, Lancaster. It was in fact Austin who was responsible for the firm's masterpieces.[15]

Paley was a founder member of the Royal Archaeological Society, a member of the Cumberland and Westmorland Antinquarian and Archaeological Society, and he took part in the meetings and excursions of both. In fact his strong historical and antiquarian interests are best to be seen in the large amount of restorations which the firm undertook. Interested in education, he was a member of the Council of the RIBA and at one time an examiner and also much involved in the work

27 Paley and Austin's offices on Castle Hill. (Geoffrey Sutcliffe)

of the Lancaster Mechanics Institute and School of Art. At the time of his death he was a Committee Member of the successor to the Mechanics Institute, the Storey Institute. In his early days he was a prominent oarsman and involved with Sharpe in the foundation of the Lancaster Rowing Club. Like many members of the extended Sharpe family of which he became a member in 1851 when he married Miss Frances Sharpe, Edmund's sister, he was interested in music and a member of the choral society.

For three years he was a member of the Borough Council, representing Queen's Ward from 1858. Nothing of great consequence took place at the time, and, unlike Sharpe, he found municipal work 'uncongenial' and at the end of his term refused to be re-nominated.[16] He did succeed Sharpe as Bridgemaster of the Hundred of South Lonsdale and as such designed the road bridge over the Lune at Caton. He was involved in various gentlemen's clubs in the town, Conservative, Reform and Liberal. He would appear to have been a gregarious person who enjoyed social clubs when he would meet people of similar interests to himself. A member of the Central Committee of the Royal Albert Asylum, he retired before being appointed architect. In the case of the Lancaster Waggon and Carriage works, of which he was a Director, he designed their extensive works with their impressive clock tower between 1863 and 1865.

His married life, like that of all of the partners, appears to have been extremely

28 The Independent (Congregational) Sunday School, Middle Street, Lancaster, 1855–6 by E. G. Paley. (Geoffrey Sutcliffe)

happy, and he and his wife with one son and three daughters lived at the Greaves, which he designed, for 'close on forty years'. He seems to have been a much loved and well respected man, his photograph suggesting a large friendly personality. It is said of him that he was 'one of nature's gentlemen therefore (who) was always cheerful and friendly'.[17] His funeral was a public one with the many attending witnessing to the esteem and popularity in which he was held by all who knew him.[18]

H. J. Austin

Hubert James Austin (1841–1915) was another son of the 'manse', being born at Redmarshall, Co Durham, the son of the Rector, the Rev. T. Austin on March 31st 1841. Educated at Richmond Grammar School, he was articled to his elder brother, Thomas, a Newcastle architect in 1860. Upon completion of his articles he joined the office of Sir George Gilbert Scott, where he remained until 1867.[19]

In 1867 Austin joined Paley, and the practice became Paley and Austin. Why did a young man with all before him in London join a practice in a town as remote as Lancaster? My researches have shown that there were already several links between Paley and the Austin family which were of long standing. In 1845, Sharpe[20] restored Redmarshall Church when Austin's father was still Rector. On this occasion, in addition to having Paley as a pupil, Sharpe also had Tom Austin working with him. This man was the eldest son of the Vicar and a good friend of E. G. Paley. Did Tom Austin, knowing that Paley was seeking a partner encourage his young half brother (whom Paley must have met as a child) to join his old friend in Lancaster?[21]

Whatever the reason for joining Paley, Austin brought to the practice great talent and energy. The firm now rapidly gained a national reputation, erecting churches, restoring ecclesiastical buildings and providing a range of other works through the North-West. Pevsner has said that Austin had 'genius'[22] and as Paley's 'brilliant partner raised (the work of the firm) to the level of the best in the country'.[23] Austin, endowed with these abilities, concentrated upon his work and took little or no part in public affairs except for being a Commissioner of Land Tax in 1886. He was not the gentleman amateur that Sharpe had been and had greater talent than Paley: he was an architect first and foremost. Like the other two men he was interested in ecclesiastical history and archaeology and was frequently sought after as an adviser in the restoration of medieval churches.

Socially he was a gifted musician and member of the Orchestral Society and of the Choral Society (both his wife and mother in law being well known local singers), as well as being fond of sketching and water colour painting.[24] A very faithful member of Lancaster's Parish Church, where he was vicar's warden for seven years and later sidesman, he superintended its alterations and renovations up to his death. The new porch, which he designed and paid for, was a memorial to his wife's parents Dr and Mrs James Langshaw. A rather reserved and authoritarian figure he nevertheless gained great pleasure from his domestic life, marrying Miss Fanny Langshaw, a niece of Edmund Sharpe, in 1870. He thus entered a large extended family to which he added five children of his own. Within the family there was much music, painting and gardening. His home, the Knoll on Westbourne Road, he designed himself and had Mawson lay out the garden. In addition he had a country home, Heversham House, and purchased Kingsworthy Court near Winchester to which he travelled each summer to sketch and paint.

H. A. Paley

Henry (Harry) Anderson Paley (1859–1946) was born in Lancaster in 1859, the eldest of four children and the only son of E. G. Paley. His mother was the former Miss Frances Sharpe and he was therefore a nephew to Edmund Sharpe. He was educated initially at the Castle Howell School in Lancaster and later at Uppingham. In 1877 he entered the family firm to begin his articles but, upon their completion, he was sent to the London office of T. E. Collcutt in 1882 'to gain wider experience'. In 1885 he was elected ARIBA and became a partner of Paley and Austin in 1886. From 1895 to 1915 he worked with H. J. Austin, but, while the practice initially had a very high reputation, by 1910, as Pevsner has pointed out, 'the zest' does appear to go out of the quality of their design work. Was Austin not a well man for some years before his death or was he too elderly to be concerned with the day to day running of the practice? Did he lose heart after the Liverpool Cathedral commission was missed?

How much of the work of the practice from 1886 to 1915 was done by Harry Paley will always be a matter of debate. Evidence suggests a heavy involvement in the Royal Lancaster Infirmary, Storey Institute and Nazareth House while drawings for St George's Stockport and the Liverpool Cathedral competition bear his name.[25] His obituary[26] records that 'with Mr Austin the firm carried out many works including about seventy five churches (plus) restorations and additions to ecclesiastical buildings'. After World War I Paley designed a number of churches, many of which were rather old fashioned and hark back to the earlier days of the firm, and a number of non-ecclesiastical works.

By the time World War II came, the practice was in the hands of men like Tarney and Baines who were elderly, and it was only one of a number of firms in the town. These included C. B. Pearson and T. H. Mawson. By now most of the work of Austin and Paley was of a local nature, being chiefly additions and alterations to buildings, often on a small scale basis.

29 Nazareth House, Lancaster 1901–2 by Austin and Paley. (Geoffrey Sutcliffe)

'Harry' Paley is still remembered in Lancaster as a kindly, jovial man, still working in 1936 at seventy seven years of age. He had a wide range of interests outside his professional career, being keenly interested in field sports, angling and shooting. He was a keen cricketer in his younger days, playing for Lancaster Cricket Club, and was a member of the Lancaster Photographic Society. For the last forty four years of his life he lived at Moorgarth in Caton but before that he lived at Halton Manor and Escowbeck Cottage.

Footnotes

1 Jenny Uglow, *Elizabeth Gaskell*, Faber and Faber, 1993.

2 There is a copy in Lancaster Reference Library.

3 In one obituary it says that he 'designed and erected some 35 churches besides a number of mansions'.

4 R. Jolley, 'Edmund Sharpe and the Pot Churches', *Architectural Review* vol. 146, December 1969.

5 RIBA Journal 150th Anniversary Issue, May 1984. 'Edmund Sharpe 1809–1877', p. 83.

6 There are copies of *The Architectural Parallels* in the Lancaster Library Collections.

7 *Lancaster Gazette*, 19 March 1836.

8 Tom Alderson, *Cricket by the Lune*, Lancaster, 1984.

9 N. Wigglesworth, *A History of Rowing in Lancaster*, Lancaster City Museums Local Studies, no. 17, 1992.

10 J. J. Gilchrist, *The Lancaster Cricket Club 1841–1909*, Lancaster, 1910.

11 According to the *DNB* on being warned that the inclusion of an illustration in one of his books might exclude him from a bishopric he is supposed to have said 'Bishop or no Bishop it shall go in'!

12 Frederick Apthorpe Paley, 1815–1888; St John's College, Cambridge 1835?–38.

13 I am indebted to Mr John Hughes for this information.

14 In the preface to the 5th edition of *Gothic Mouldings* by F. E. Paley, a letter from E. G. Paley is quoted in which he says that 'my brother, I recollect well read this work (Rickman's *Attempt to Discriminate the Styles of Architecture in England*) with avidity and became extremely interested in the subject of English Architecture'. The date is between 1839 and 1842, the time of E. G. Paley's articles with Sharpe.

15 N. Pevsner, *The Buildings of England, North Lancashire, op cit.*, p. 31.

16 His obituary says 'he devoted himself to his practice and that prevented his taking any prominent public position', *Lancaster Observer*, 25 Jan. 1895.

17 Obituary, *op cit.*

18 Obituary, *op cit.*

19 An attachment to one of the major offices (like Scott) gave a young man at the beginning of his career a distinct advantage. *The Victorian Church*, ed. C. Brooks and A. Saint, p. 176.

20 Personal communication from Peter Meadows.

21 T. Austin redesigned Redmarshall Church in 1857.

22 N. Pevsner, *The Buildings of England, South Lancashire, op cit.*, p. 44.

23 N. Pevsner, *The Buildings of England, Cheshire*, p. 36.

24 He had been first secretary of the Spring Garden Sketch Club while in London and was editor of the *John o'Gaunt Sketch Book* produced in three volumes between 1874 and 1885.

25 RIBA Drawings Collection.

26 Journal of the RIBA, July 1946.

4
Church building in the nineteenth century

The growth of church building

It is for church architecture rather than for their secular buildings that Victorian architects are best known. This generalisation is as true of Sharpe, Paley and Austin as it is of Bodley, Street or Scott. The three Lancaster men had a practice which began in the year before Victoria's accession and produced most of its best work before her death in 1901. During this particular and unique period in the last century, with all of its tumultuous social and economic changes, churches provided architects with vast numbers of commissions. This Lancaster firm was no exception, churches providing their largest single source of work, around 40 per cent of their commissions.

In many cases this meant that a completely new church was erected to their designs, but in numerous other examples they added portions like a new vestry or porch. Again, some churches were restored to overcome the ravages of time, others because the incumbent, attracted to the Oxford Movement, required it to be altered it to fit the needs of particular liturgical practices. Restoration could be total or partial, many of the latter being the replacement of the chancel. As Pevsner noted, few churches avoided the 'Restorers' before Ruskin led the reaction to their activities. Thus, while much of their work was done for Low/Evangelical congregations, the new chancel may either be evidence of the Oxford Movement[1] or just part of widespread feeling on the part of the clergy that a new larger chancel was needed for worship.

In looking at our towns and villages, one is immediately struck, like Betjeman, by the sheer number of churches erected in the period 1820–1900.[2] There were two main reasons for this. Firstly there was the enormous growth in population and consequently of towns, the result of the Industrial Revolution; secondly there was the religious revival of the last century.

The population of England and Wales rose rapidly from nine million in 1801 to reach thirty two million in 1901. At the same time the percentage of the population living in towns grew from 33 per cent to nearly 80 per

30 The entrance to the Lancaster Waggon works, 1864–5 by E. G. Paley. (Geoffrey Sutcliffe)

31 The Royal Lancaster Infirmary, 1893–6 by Paley, Austin and Paley. (Geoffrey Sutcliffe)

cent. Individual towns grew rapidly, initially from in-migration and later, when the major health hazards had been overcome, by the resident population increasing itself. (see Table V).

It was in providing churches for these rapidly growing populations that architects found much work. The creation of new parishes had taken place in a small way in the previous century but Peel's New Parishes Act (1843) allowed their creation on a large scale. Along with a new parish went the need for a church. This could be a new one or the adaptation of an existing chapel of ease.[3] A growth in population could lead to the extending of the old parish church.

Between 1840 and 1876 the Anglicans built 1727 new churches in England and Wales and rebuilt, or restored, or enlarged a further 7144 existing medieval churches. This cost £25,548,703! Manchester, a new diocese, built 193; Ripon, also created to serve an industrial area, 182. Between 1868 and 1880 seventy new parishes were created per year, and as late as 1880–1900 thirty five per year. From 1876 to 1911 a further 2159 churches and chapels were added.[4]

All of the men in the Lancaster practice were Anglicans (two being sons of the clergy) and it is not surprising that they gained from this church building boom. On the other hand there was also an enormous growth in non-conformity[5] and Roman Catholicism, and in the earlier days of the practice chapels and churches were designed for both.[6] In fact St Peter's Church, Lancaster, which is Paley's finest work was designed for the Roman Catholics, and it is now a cathedral.

Table V
Population increases of selected industrial towns and cities, 1801–1901

	1801	1831	1851	1871	1891	1901†
Manchester	*75,252	*235,000	335,640	*425,241	503,368	543,872
Liverpool	*78,000	*210,000	*275,955	*493,405	517,980	684,958
Birmingham	*74,000	*144,000	*242,260	*367,477	478,113	523,204
Leeds	*53,000	*123,000	*172,270	*259,212	367,505	429,000
Blackburn	*12,000	27,091	*52,187	*85,579	120,064	127,626
Preston	30,000	33,112	*70,309	*87,291	107,573	112,989
Barrow	c65	c65	*1000	*18,911	51,712	57,586
Accrington	3,077	6,283	10,374	21,788	38,603	43,122

(* estimated by 1891 Census Table 9)
† C. B. Phillips and J. H. Smith, *Lancashire and Cheshire from* AD *1540*, Longman, 1994.

The second reason for the growth in church building is because of a genuine religious revival at this time. This resulted in a demand for new churches as well as meeting the needs of the increasing population. The possibility of such an occurrence taking place would have seemed unlikely at the beginning of the century 'with the Church of England ... ill prepared to meet the challenge of a new day'.[7] Although there were shining examples amongst those of an Evangelical persuasion who led good lives and had a high sense of social responsibility, much was wrong in church and society. There was moral decline, even at the highest levels of society. Morality had sunk to a low ebb in the time of the Prince Regent and this continued when he was King as George IV. The Anglican church was still suffering from the decline begun in the previous century. All Christians were nominally members of it, even if they were nonconformist. The Church of England was identified by many as being too closely tied to State and Establishment, and both clergy and bishops were unpopular. The latter with their ingrained conservatism opposed change at all costs and their voting against the Reform Bill led to their effigies being burned and to them being threatened. Pluralism and absenteeism were rife, with 3699 clergymen being legally non resident in 1808 and 2446 illegally! (This had reduced to 1033 illegally in 1815). Pluralism was partly due to the low incomes many clergymen received, making it necessary to have several benefices at once. It was even worse for the resident curate who might, if he was lucky, have £30–40 per annum but could have as little as £5. In the case of rich livings, nepotism took place, and most were in the hands of rich and aristocratic families. Many churches were in a sad state of repair and there were too few seats in the rapidly growing towns, thus Manchester in 1818 had 11,000 seats for 80,000 people, and Sheffield 6,300 for 55,000!

The work of Wesley in the eighteenth century had not produced the revival he had expected in the Church of England but had led to the creation of a new rapidly growing denomination which now posed a threat to Anglicanism. Reform had to come from the Church of England itself. It was the Evangelicals who, by organising a petition, obtained government support and were instrumental in the setting up of the Church Building Society in 1818. As the *Quarterly Review* of that year said 'the edifices which we have erected are manufacturies and prisons; the former producing tenants for the latter. The only way of making them good subjects is by making them good Christians'.[8] The creation of the Commissioners' Churches with the one

32 The Royal Albert Hospital, Lancaster 1868-73 with the superb central tower by H. J. Austin. (Geoffrey Sutcliffe)

and a half million pounds of government grants was not merely a disinterested and charitable act, it was also the Established Church fighting back. A memorandum sent to the Prime Minister in 1815 had drawn attention to the dangers to which 'the constitution of this country is exposed for want of places of worship particularly persons of middle and lower classes'. Parliament identified with, and spoke for, the Church of England and saw an obvious threat to the country if more Anglican churches were not built.

Later in the century there was a genuine spiritual revival within the church, a revitalisation of parish life and the emergence of an educated and trained clergy, alive to the social problems of the country and their role in their amelioration. There was the growth in the 1840s of the Oxford Movement (otherwise known as the Tractarians and Puseyites) which affected the High Church but operated in affluent and poor areas alike. The Low Church or Broad Movement with its Evangelical wing and close affinities with the Nonconformist and Methodists flourished too, building new churches and extending others, though in different ways to the Tractarians. At the same time Nonconformists and Catholics flourished. The results were the same, whatever the cause: in town and city new parishes were created and churches sprang up, while in the country many chapels of ease now gained parochial status.

Given these two phenomena, population growth and a revival in religion, it is not surprising that churches were erected in great numbers from 1818 to the end of the century. In any average industrial town, as Betjeman noted, the vast majority of its churches date from the second half of the last century. 'Oldest will be the Parish Church probably medieval. Next there will be a late Georgian church built by the Commissioners. Then there will be three built between 1850 and 1870, and three 1870–1900'.[9] This generalisation is true of most of the North West, and the practice was well placed to obtain many commissions during this growth in church numbers.

It should not be thought that Paley and Austin only did ecclesiastical work. Certainly in the period after 1850, when new country houses were being built or extended, they carried out a number of commissions as well as a full range of secular buildings. The practice was however pre-eminently a firm of ecclesiastical architects and was recognised as such by its contemporaries. The bulk of Sharpe's work is churches upward of forty while in the obituaries of Paley and Austin particular mention is made of their role as church architects. However it should be noted that the emphasis upon churches at the expense of other work is a fairly late phenomenon and may be due to the arrival of Austin in the practice. While Paley seems to have been willing to take on a variety of work, Austin seems to have been involved in little secular work except for middle-class houses. It has in fact been suggested by some people that when Austin arrived he specialised in the churches and Paley did whatever secular work was required. However, an office like theirs must have had a full range of work, ranging in scale from a memorial cross, single house or shop, through a railway commission to a large country house. It is this sort of minor work which still remains to be discovered. In many cases the principal partners may have played little part in the designing of these small commissions which

33 The Storey Institute, Lancaster, 1887–91 by Paley, Austin and Paley. (Geoffrey Sutcliffe)

34 St Thomas's Church, Lancaster, 1839–40 by Edmund Sharpe. (Geoffrey Sutcliffe)

were left to their pupils and juniors. The large and prestigious works appear in their obituaries but a lot of work still remains to be done in identifying the small but nevertheless important work undertaken by the practice.

The ecclesiastical styles of the practice

During the course of the century different styles in ecclesiastical architecture developed. These can be summarised as essentially a move away from a pre-archaeological style[10] which is only loosely medieval in derivation and which was used for the Commissioners' churches, to a more accurate and 'correct' Gothic from the 1840s onwards. This change owes much to the work of Pugin, the ecclesiologists[11] and to a number of practising architects with an interest in historical architecture. They produced books containing accurate measured drawings of medieval buildings.[12] The effect of all of these is known as the 'Gothic Revival' which continued through the High Victorian fashion. This movement held sway for much of the rest of the century, albeit adapted by particular architects and in the design of churches in different locations as shown in St George's, Stockport, designed by Austin.

In 1818, as has been seen, the Church Building Society was founded by the Evangelical Movement. The Society began its work with large subscriptions including one from the King and encouraged Parliament to grant one million pounds as a national thanksgiving for the victory at Waterloo (the churches then built are in fact sometimes called Waterloo Churches). With this and a further half-million grant of 1824 a large number of so-called Commissioners' churches were built for the working classes in those urban areas with rapidly growing populations. In the case of the ninety six which resulted from the first grant from the Lords Commissioners of the Treasury and which cost £5000 to £15,000, the Commissioners paid for them all, but the 450 later ones got an average grant of 10 per cent. This meant that most of their money was raised from private individuals. In all some £6 million was spent on church building between 1818 and 1833. Of the ninety-six Waterloo churches (pre 1830) nineteen were in Lancashire and sixteen in Yorkshire; of the second grant (1830–56) it was sixty-three and ninety respectively.

The young Edmund Sharpe, newly established in Lancaster, was well placed for such work. Through his cousin the Rev John William Whittaker, Vicar of Blackburn, he obtained eight commissions in the Blackburn area. His first three buildings were all essays in the Romanesque style, popular in the pre-archaeological phase and something he had studied on his European travels. They were St Mark's, Witton 1836–8; St Saviour's, Bamber Bridge 1836–8 and Christ Church, Chatburn 1838.

The next five were all in a Gothic style which was the norm for the Commissioners. Holy Trinity, Morecambe, like the others, has a long narrow 'body', lancet windows and a tower with pinnacles and crockets. In this pre Tractarian phase the church lacked aisles and had only a small chancel. Such churches were essentially preaching halls for the working classes. No one would mistake them for medieval buildings with their 'lean pointed lancet windows' though they are perhaps 'Early English, if they must have a historical label'.[13]

By the 1840s these and similar churches were already dated in appearance, for this was the decade of the 'great divide' in Victorian

35 St Matthew's and St James' Church, Mossley, Liverpool, 1870–75 by Paley and Austin.

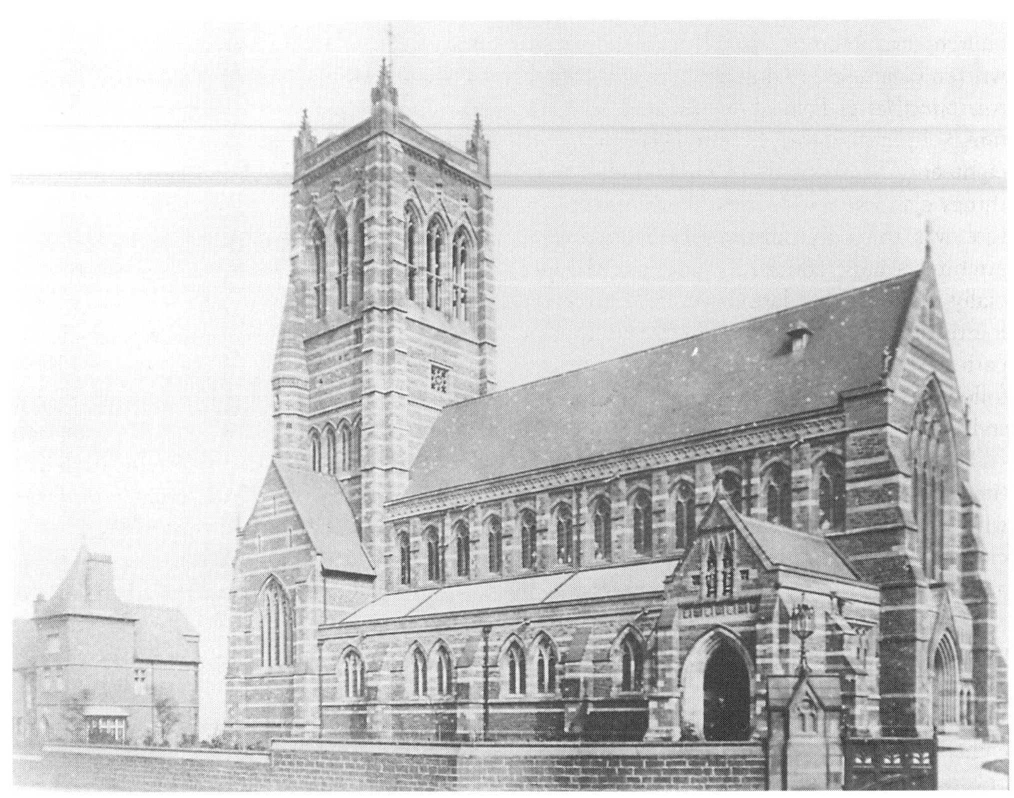

36 St Matthew's and St James' Church, 1870–75 by Paley and Austin. An original photograph of around 1875.

37 St Stephen's Church, Whalley, Wigan, 1930–38, by H. A. Paley.

church architecture. In 1836 Pugin had written *Contrasts*[14] and in 1841 published *The true principles of Pointed or Christian Architecture*.[15] In the latter he attacked false (or eighteenth century) Gothic as well as all things classical. In his view Gothic architecture was the only architecture for worship. Architects must adhere to Gothic and especially that of the late thirteenth to early fourteenth centuries. Churches built to this pattern should be architecturally accurate and follow faithfully the Geometric Decorated style.

The call made by Pugin, who was by this time a Catholic, was taken up by the group who formed the Cambridge Camden Society.[16] Their journal *The Ecclesiologist* aimed to show architects how to design in this the correct style. 'It is the combination of Pugin's combative writings and the Ecclesiologists' praise and criticism which shaped English church architecture from the eighteen forties to the eighteen seventies and beyond.[17]

Edmund Sharpe himself designed two buildings which herald the Gothic Revival but it was left to Paley, both working alone and in partnership with Austin, to realise the great glories of the firm.

Pevsner has summarised this phrase viz.

> The change which took place in this one firm in the 1840s is a national one – from a Gothic true only in an associational sense ie with motifs that suggest Gothic, to a Gothic archaeologically sufficiently accurate to make the layman think he is looking at a real medieval building ... in the Middle Pointed or Second Pointed ... the style, characterised by geometrical tracery forms up to and excluding the flowing of the Decorated style.[18]

Sharpe was to gain the gold medal of RIBA, not for his own designs but because of his historical writings. He produced a large number of works on medieval architecture including the *Architectural Parallels*, which are measured drawings of actual churches and abbeys. He was pre-eminently a scholar of the Decorated period and it is not surprising that his St Mary the Virgin in Knowsley (1843–4) is in the Decorated style, as is the spire of Kirkham Parish Church. This latter is probably his best work and makes one wonder what he might have achieved in architecture if he had not been seduced by railways!

From 1838 to 1851 Paley worked closely with Sharpe and during this time he obviously learned a great deal from him, both in the field of design and the practicalities of running a practice. Drawings exist in the RIBA collections and in Lancaster, made by Paley at this time and he also lithographed some of the Sharpe plates. It is not surprising then, that Paley accepted and practised the tenets of the Gothicists, particularly as an Anglican and the son and grandson of clergymen. His elder brother Frederick, a Cambridge lecturer and member of the Camden Society, was also an authority on medieval architecture.[19]

Between 1851 and 1865 Paley designed a large number of churches and restored others. In the main he followed the Decorated style or something closely resembling it. His best design is for St Peter's Cathedral, Lancaster which was designed in the style of 1300, and was erected in 1857–9. This is a fine building with a 'high excellently detailed north west steeple' (Pevsner) which I can see glinting in the strong March sun as I write. One might almost take it for a 'genuine' medieval building with 'correct' tracery, for example on the north side of the nave and the later rose window on the south transept. Almost as fine is St George's Church, Barrow 1859–61, a large church of slate and red sandstone with a massive tower.

Paley did much other work but little of it has the quality of these two buildings. Most of his other churches are not very special and Pevsner stated that even his Bolton Parish Church is 'confident if conventional', not as enterprising as Paley and Austin were going to be.[20]

In 1868 when H. J. Austin joined Paley the

character of the architecture changes with a new found 'nobility and resourcefulness'[21] which had not been seen in the bulk of buildings designed by Paley alone. The first products of the partnership were St James' Church, Barrow with its beautiful steeple and internal brick arches, and though, not strictly ecclesiastical, the fine French Chateau style tower with which they completed the frontage of the Royal Albert Hospital, Lancaster. This tower, not surprisingly given Austin's earlier career, bears some resemblance to that on Scott's St Pancras Station Hotel designed in 1865.

Now designs for large and small church poured from their offices. Many of the best are in south Lancashire. Christ Church, Widnes; St Chad's, Kirkby; St Matthew's and St James', Mossley Hill. St Mary's, Dalton is a fine one in the North, as are Pilling and Flookburgh. It is not only their large churches that are fine; the small ones at Torver and Finsthwaite (the mountain churches) and at Dolphinholme rival anything Bodley or Street could do.

Between 1868 and the death of Austin in 1915 there was a prodigious output of buildings especially new churches and restorations. This output slackened around 1900, probably due to a slackening in demand rather than to any failure in design. By the turn of the century the great church boom was all but over, most of those needed in the cities having been built. However it must be said that the zest was going out of the firm by this time and that their designs were looking somewhat dated. Later, Harry Paley designed a number of churches and restored others. For the majority of these he returned to the styles prevalent at the turn of the century. Even though he was successful in some cases, for example at Bilsborrow, in others he appears dated and old fashioned. St Stephen's Church, Blackpool (1927) is a more exciting design and an honourable exception to these generalisations. By the time Harry Paley retired in 1936 there can have been few Church commissions. Ironically, had the practice survived the Second World War with new partners, there would have been new work either in restoring the ravages of the war or designing new churches for the estates on the edges of the towns.

39 An internal view of St Mary's Church, Widnes, looking west.

During the great days of the practice from 1868–1915, whatever its changes of name, the partners designed many fine buildings. If Austin had the 'genius', Paley was thorough, workmanlike and was always a follower of the Gothic Revival. Much of their joint output is interesting and attractive as well as being distinctive. After a time the student of their work comes to recognise it even in a building visited for the first time.

One is bound to ask what is it that makes their work so distinctive? The overall effects are exciting and resourceful while there are many fine details. Yet the end product is never fussy nor eclectic but rather crisp, clean and precise. Their designs have superbly detailed towers (often with a stair turret) and finely designed tracery. All of their churches are in a Gothic style sufficiently accurate for us to think today we are looking at a medieval church. They range from a Decorated style

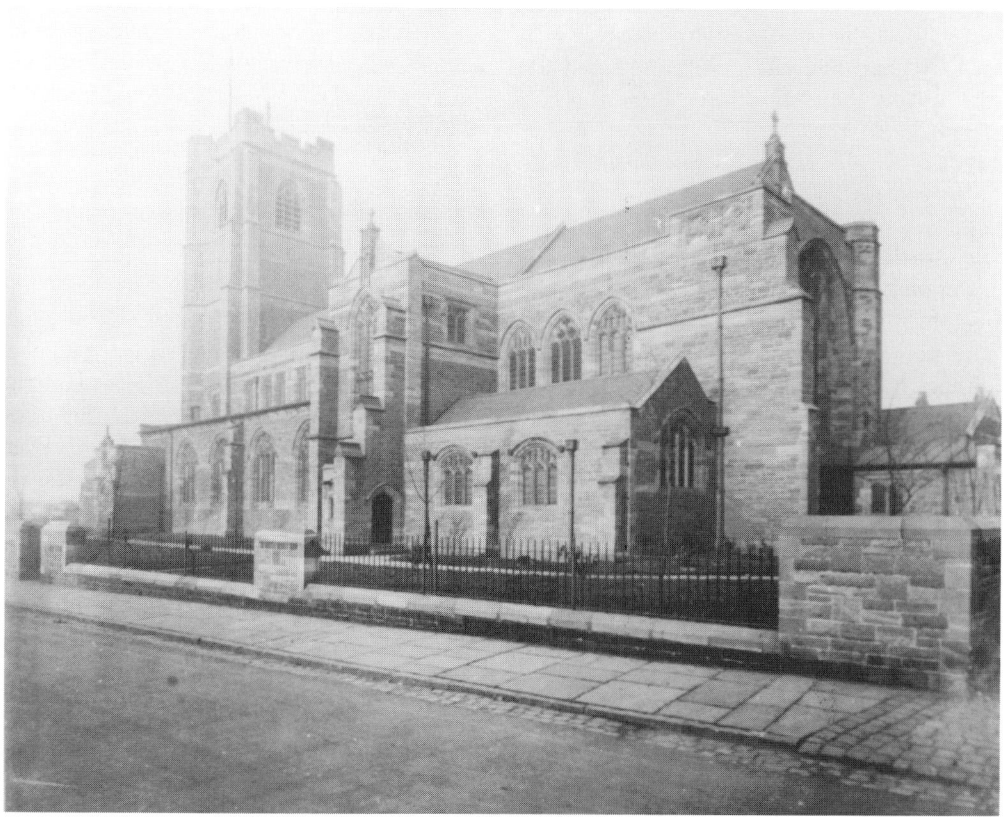

38 St Mary's Church, Widnes, 1908–18, by Paley and Austin.

through a free Decorated style to a Perpendicular one. They made use of both stone and brick and the reddish Runcorn stone was a favourite of theirs. In many of their buildings they used sandstone which gives a pinkish mushroom colour to the buildings for example Atherton while elsewhere they used a yellow stone. In common with many Victorian church architects they used polychrome effects of different coloured stone and brickwork often with a chequer board design. Externally one often recognises their work by the high transepts and the fine quality of the stonework. It is an interesting exercise to look at one of their drawings, these are more like engineering designs, so clear and precise are they, with a sharp cut-off effect especially at the east end. Normally the porches of their churches are at the extreme west end.[22]

Internally one common distinctive feature is the way the two sides of the chancel and even the nave are different. At Broughton one side of the chancel has windows, the other an arcade and passage. They never repeat themselves and they are always resourceful and 'interesting' according to Pevsner.

Some of their churches are superb, notably St Matthew's and St James' Church, Mossley Hill, Christ Church, Waterloo and the magnificent St George's Church, Stockport. These last two have a precision and sharpness about them that is a far cry from the worst excesses of Gothic Revival. As Pevsner says of St George's it is 'nationally speaking a masterpiece of the latest historicism, designed just before the most original younger English architects begin to turn away from the strict Gothic Revival'.[23] It shows what Austin was capable of (in 1900 Austin and Paley won a

Silver Medal at the Paris Exhibition: was it for this?) and how the practice spanned the full range of the Gothic Revival, from beginning to end.

All of their work is of a high quality, and in an obituary of H. A. Paley they are paid the compliment that their style 'was a northern version of Bodley, following after the Decorated and Perpendicular styles'.

Perhaps it is possible to speak of a Lancaster school. It is not only the designs which are first rate but also the execution of them. Internally they made great use of James Hatch of Lancaster for their woodwork, bought encaustic tiles from Staffordshire and roofing tiles from Ruabon and used a number of craftsmen for metal work. The firm of Shrigley and Hunt did stained glass and other work.

In the matter of Church decoration they avoided the worst excesses of the High Church school, and, as Anson[24] has said

> Their furnishings are all honest and conscientious and whatever may be lacking in their interiors they express the temperament of the average Lancashire or Yorkshire worshipper ... [their] pulpits, choir stalls, fonts and communion tables being generally designed for moderate Anglican ceremonial.

In fact drawings exist of examples of all of these which were done as individual items or as part of a larger commission.

What then of High Anglican ceremonial? The 1840s saw the development of the Oxford Movement which required specific church buildings suited to their particular forms of worship. This was obviously easier in a new church, but an old one could be

adapted. The reformers of the Oxford Movement were particularly anxious to alter the internal arrangements of churches which had, in their eyes, become preaching houses. They wanted a less dominant pulpit and a church uncluttered by galleries and pews, to facilitate greater emphasis on the Eucharist and to accommodate more ceremonial in the service. They also favoured symbolism as is shown by their liking for a cruciform church.

Given the importance of the Eucharist and the subsequent role of the altar and its surroundings there was a need for the altar to be at the extreme east end. The altar was

40, 41 (*opposite*) All Saint's Church, Hertford, 1895–1905, by Austin and Paley, a southern foray for the practice!

42 St Saviour's Church, Bolton by Paley and Austin. Built 1882–5; demolished 1975.

often elaborate, perhaps with a reredos. It carried candles and a cross, and it was raised above the level of the chancel by three steps. The chancel itself had to be longer and bigger than before in order to contain the sanctuary with the altar and choir. (It was from here that the priest took most of the service.) Also the chancel was to be above the level of the nave and separated from it by an open screen. The nave usually had the pulpit at the east side and had a central aisle and often side aisles to allow for processions. There was low open seating rather than box pews, allowing the congregation to see the altar, and the font was situated at the west end near the door to symbolise the entry to God's Kingdom.

In addition to all these modifications many High Anglicans reintroduced vestments, which had disappeared with the Reformation, and caused many churches to be sumptuously decorated with works of art, tiles, beautiful cloths, stained glass, wood and metal goods. This work was often concentrated in the chancel around the altar.

All of the evidence available to us appears to confirm the statements of Anson regarding the church interiors executed by the firm. The normal church commission which the practice obtained was for a middle of the road type of congregation. As Coleman[25] has pointed out in Lancashire where they obtained the bulk of their commissions, Tractarianism had rather less popular sympathy. Unlike other industrial areas, Evangelical Anglicanism was better fitted to the mood here. Their buildings provide little evidence of High Anglicanism. There is glass, good wood and metal designs and generally open pews. Sometimes there is a central aisle but in others like St Paul's Church, Scotforth there are side aisles only to specifically prevent processions.

Restoration work

It is to the firm's work as restorers that we now turn. Restoration was done to repair a church or the opportunity was taken to do it when it was necessary to extend a building or adapt it to meet the needs of the new liturgy. Whatever the particular reasons, the four men did a good deal of restoration work and this type of work was an important part of their practice. The reasons for this must include the reputation of the founder, Edmund Sharpe, as a leading authority on medieval buildings. Paley, in addition to learning from Sharpe, was a noted antiquarian himself and a founder member of the British Archaeological Society. His sketch books show him to have had a lively and educated interest in architectural styles. Austin too was interested in these topics, as his

43 St George's Church, Stockport, 1893–97 by Paley, Austin and Paley.

work at St Mary's, Lancaster in 1911, when he unearthed the remains of an eastern apse, shows. Thus all three were both interested and knowledgeable. Sharpe was a noted church restorer. Of Austin it was said 'as an adviser his skill was eagerly sought (for church restoration) on account of his life long study and exceptional knowledge of the ancient ecclesiastical buildings of this country'.[26]

It is obvious that even in the last century there was more than one view about restoration. Some like Scott felt that by removing furnishings and ornaments from later periods than the medieval and in some cases replacing parts of the buildings themselves they were restoring churches to their original form. In this we can see the work of Pugin and the Ecclesiologists. Unfortunately many dreadful acts were done in the name of restoration, and a second school of thought developed which held the view that conservation rather than restoration should be the aim. John Ruskin and William Morris were two conservationists. In 1874 Ruskin refused the Gold Medal of the RIBA because of the 'destruction under the name of restoration brought about by architects'.

When one looks at the works of restoration done by Paley and Austin it is necessary to admit having an ambivalent attitude to them. How many churches were in imminent danger of collapse and needed 'rebuilding'? Many churches still stand of the same age as those largely demolished and rebuilt. However faithful the design, we still have a nineteenth century church! The people of Wigan Parish Church wished to keep it, yet in its restoration it was just about rebuilt. It is probable that it would not have fallen down. At a smaller scale what was lost in the way of furnishings and woodwork as architects sought to reconstruct a medieval church? Anything from the fifteenth century onwards was fair game. There is evidence from photographs and drawings of buildings before their restoration of what we have lost. The work of Lord Grimthorpe at St Albans may be the worst but even Scott felt it necessary to defend himself against critics later on in life. A visit to Kirkby Lonsdale which was restored by Paley and Austin in the 1870s presents a very different picture from a church like Whitby or Melling. These retain something of their original character. At best, restored churches are a tidy, neat, antiseptic version of what the Victorians felt such a medieval church should look like. At worst, all of the accumulated artefacts of centuries, which made them appear crowded and untidy but which were an integral part of their history, were swept away in the name of progress. Paley and Austin were no different from many but better than most. As Pevsner says 'there are few churches in the country which (were) not restored on Camdenian principles before the 1840s and the time when Ruskin and Morris's influence checked them'.[27] All of the evidence we have suggests that Paley and Austin restoration work was done sensitively and with care. There are no stories to suggest artistic vandalism or excessive and over zealous removal of existing features. In this as in all things they were sensible and restrained.

Footnotes

1 The Oxford Movement was a movement for reforming the life and worship of the Church of England. It resulted from the famous Assize Sermon preached by John Keble in 1833 in St Mary's Church, Oxford. An essential feature was the restoration of some of the ceremonial and worship which had fallen into complete disuse since the Reformation. There was too a strong architectural movement within it.

2 J. Betjeman (ed.), *Collins Guide to Parish Churches of England and Wales*, Collins, 1980.

3 A chapel-at-ease was a building used for religious worship which was erected for the ease of those inhabitants in an outlying part of a parish and far away from the parish church.

Such chapels were served by curates and often had rights of baptism, marriage and burial.

4 *The Victorian Church*, Brooks and Saint, *op cit.*

5 In the 1851 religious census over 40 per cent attending services were non-conformists.

6 Other denominational church building also increased. For England, Wales and Scotland, Methodist churches grew from 6649 to 8606 (1851–1909 (31% increase)); Congregational chapels 3244–4652 (1851–1909 (43% increase)); Baptist chapels 2082–3047 (1861–1911 (46% increase)); Roman Catholic (England and Wales) 570–1592 (1851–1900 (168% increase)).

7 K. S. Latourette, *Christianity in a Revolutionary Age: A History of Christianity in the Nineteenth and Twentieth Centuries*, Harper and Brothers, New York, 1959.

8 N. Pevsner, *The Building of England, North Lancashire*, Penguin, 1969.

9 J. Betjeman (ed.), *op. cit.*

10 Pre-archaeological is the term used for churches built before the work of Pugin and the ecclesiologists and the Gothic Revival. Such churches have a Gothic 'feel' to them but their designs are not closely based on medieval examples. From the 1830s there was a more serious archaeological and architectural correctness about church design. Now churches were designed in correct and accurate Gothic styles, the so called Gothic Revival.

11 See footnotes 1 and 16 on the Oxford Movement and Camden Society.

12 E.g. Shaw, Nesfield, Street.

13 N. Pevsner *The Buildings of England, South Lancashire, op cit.*

14 A. W. N. Pugin, *Contrasts for a Parallel Between the Noble Edifices of the Middle Ages and Corresponding Buildings of the Present Day: showing the present decay of taste*, Dolman, London, 1836.

15 There are three main styles of Gothic in England (according to Rickman):

(1) First Pointed also known as the Early English style. This flourished from the late twelfth century to the end of the thirteenth.

(2) Second or Middle Pointed, also known as the Decorated style. From the late thirteenth until the second half of the fourteenth century.

(3) Third Pointed, or the Perpendicular style. From the middle of the fourteenth century into the sixteenth century.

16 In 1839 the Oxford Society for promoting the study of Gothic Society (The Gothic Society) and the Cambridge Camden Society, renamed after 1846 the Ecclesiological Society, were founded. The Camden Society or Ecclesiologists exercised enormous influence in the building of new churches and the restoration of old ones, believing that not only was Gothic the true style but that its best period was the late thirteenth and early fourteenth centuries, the decorated or Middle Pointed period.

17 N. Pevsner, *The Buildings of England, South Lancashire*, p. 32.

18 N. Pevsner, *The Buildings of England, North Lancashire*, p. 31.

19 F. A. Paley (1815–1888) was for a time Honorary Secretary of the Camden Society. In 1845 he published *The Church Restorer: a tale treating of Ancient and Modern Architecture and Church Decoration* as well as *Gothic Mouldings*.

20 N. Pevsner, *The Buildings of England, South Lancashire*, p. 79.

21 N. Pevsner, op. cit., *North Lancashire*, p. 33.

22 Personal communication by Michael Bottomley.

23 N. Pevsner, *The Buildings of England, Cheshire*, Penguin, 1971.

24 P. F. Anson, *Fashions in Church Furnishinngs 1840–1940*, Studio-Vista, London, 1960.

25 B. I. Coleman, *The Church in the Nineteenth Century: A Social Geography*, Historical Association, 1980.

26 Obituary of H. J. Austin, *The Lancaster Guardian*, 27 March 1915.

27 N. Pevsner, *Some Architectural Writers of the Nineteenth Century*, Clarendon Press, Oxford 1972.

44 St George's Church, Stockport.

5
An analysis of the buildings produced by the practice

During the century-long existence of this firm the partners designed a vast corpus of buildings and undertook a wide range of commissions, great and small. The purpose of this chapter is to analyse this work in terms of the type of commissions undertaken, the scale of them, and their geographical location. Following on from a general overview of the output of Sharpe and the several partnerships, there is a detailed analysis of the period 1851–1895 when first Paley worked alone and later Paley and Austin were in partnership together. This period of forty-four years is essentially what people mean when they talk about Paley and Austin. In fact, their partnership only lasted twenty seven years and for the last nine years together they were joined by Harry Paley. This however is the period when one or both of the main partners was actively involved in the practice and can be seen today as the firm's 'golden' period.

The detailed analysis of information or data collected from primary/documentary sources and by fieldwork has long been the concern of a number of disciplines including the social sciences. Geographers particularly have been interested in collecting appropriate information, processing it (using mathematical and statistical techniques) and presenting it by the use of graphical techniques including mapping. Maps and diagrams have always been of central importance where studies have been made which require the visual presentations of data. Thus it is possible by means of a line graph to detail the growth or decline of the output of a product; by use of a columnar graph to show the different categories of a phenomenon or the changes in the distribution of that phenomenon over time.

Obviously the use of maps to reveal the spatial pattern of a set of data is common to many subjects including History and Economics as well as Geography. It does not appear however to have been the practice of most architectural historians to make wide use of these techniques or to process and analyse their information about a particular architect in this way. When studies of individuals have been undertaken, the authors content themselves with giving the total output of an architect, e.g. Scott 750, or sometimes with providing a list of their works. Thus in '*Seven Victorian Architects*'[1] each of the contributors appends a list of the 'chief works' of the architect they have written about; as does Cole for Scott.[2] What analysis is carried out is chiefly stylistic and then usually for the ecclesiastical works only. There is no attempt to analyse the output of a man by the type of work he carried out, the scale of each commission (in terms of whether it is a new building, a restoration, or a mere alteration/addition) or spatially.

There is however no intrinsic reason why the task of applying such graphical and cartographic techniques cannot be carried out upon the works of an architect. If a reasonably complete set of data exists then it is a straightforward job to analyse it in this way. The fact is that when this analysis has been carried out the resultant maps and graphs provide us with fresh insights into the work of an architectural practice.

What follows is an attempt to use this approach in order to analyse the work carried out by E. Sharpe, E. G. Paley, H. J. Austin and H. J. Paley from 1836 to 1942. The result is an analytical study of the work of the four men which is presented as a contribution to the historical geography of the firm and

45 All Saint's Church, Hertford, 1895–1905 by Austin and Paley.

provides a view of the spatial effect and impact of a major regional practice.

In 1944 according to a number of Lancaster people, including one who was a witness to part of the exercise (Harold Jackson) the entire contents of the Austin and Paley's office were taken to the tip or salvaged for waste paper. Except for a few items which escaped this wholesale destruction, the complete records of the practice (including the Liverpool Cathedral Competition drawings) were destroyed. In the absence of these records it has been necessary for people interested in the history of the firm to use a variety of other sources in order to create a list of their architectural works. It is this list which is used for the subsequent analysis of their work and serves as the basis of Appendix A.

These sources range in order of their significance from the obituaries of the four men in the local newspapers of the period via the holdings of the Lancaster Library, the various County Records offices and the RIBA drawings collection, to the odd snippet gathered from a conversation or a chance find. In addition to public collections there are a number of items in private hands especially drawings and sketch books. Finally there are the plans and drawings which remain with the buildings themselves. All of the sources that have been discovered so far have been utilised in constructing the list of their works, though it is likely that other small collections of material await discovery.

The best single source, and that by definition contemporary, is the various obituaries in the local newspapers. These give details both of their private lives and their commissions. Each of the four had one or more, often lengthy obituaries in Lancaster newspapers; *The Guardian*, *Observer* and *Gazette*, as well as in professional journals like *The Builder*.[3] In each case they provide a list of

46 Christ Church, Waterloo, 1891–9 by Paley, Austin and Paley.

their major works. The obituary of Edmund Sharpe published in the *Lancaster Guardian*[4] unusually gives no details of his architectural works but another[5] states that he 'designed thirty five churches besides a number of Mansions'. E. G. Paley's obituaries are remarkably detailed and the information must have been supplied by the office. That in the *Lancaster Observer*[6] has a list of seventy two buildings he designed alone plus 'forty new churches and other buildings' he had done while in partnership with H. J. Austin'. The *Lancaster Guardian*[7] described how he had designed and created 'episcopal churches costing £300,000 in the Lancaster area alone'.

The obituary of Hubert Austin[8] says that he 'designed over one hundred new churches and (carried out) a still greater amount of restoration and additions to existing medieval churches' plus domestic works; while the *Lancaster Observer* lists[9] many of the churches. When Harry Paley died in 1946 the July edition of the RIBA Journal stated that he had carried out with H. J. Austin about seventy five churches plus restorations and additions. Some of these churches are named and there is mention of some non-ecclesiastical work like the Royal Lancaster Infirmary and the Nurses Home. Certainly, by adding together all of the detail from these obituaries we have a sound start to the task of creating a list of their works.

A second major source of information is provided by the various collections of material which exist and relate to the firm. Within Lancaster there are two, though neither is really substantial. The first and larger (much of which was given by Mrs H. A. Paley) is held by the Lancaster Library. There are several sketch books, a number of scrap books collected by Mr Roper which contain material and three volumes of architectural sketches and details which largely consist of fixtures rather than buildings. There is a sketchbook,

47 St John the Baptist, Atherton, 1878–80, by Paley and Austin.

containing sketches by E. G. Paley and a collection of photographs and drawings, some of which are from journals like *The Builder*.

A smaller collection is in the Lancaster Museum and contains a number of drawings of Ripley Hospital and Chapel.[10] Recently Mr Basil Austin has deposited a small collection of materials relating to the Austin family with the Museum; as has Mr Colin Stansfield.

The other major collection of material is in London. The drawings collection of the RIBA is located in Portman Square and contains a number of drawings and plans produced by the four men. They include a group of topographical drawings, some drawings done for Edmund Sharpe's *Architectural Parallels* as well as various designs for commissions. Thus there are drawings for the St Michael's, Coventry, Bell Tower of 1891, which was never built, and some materials for the Liverpool Cathedral competition and St George's, Stockport. These drawings which cover all of the partnerships from Sharpe onwards were mostly presented to the RIBA by Mrs H. A. Paley via Mr J. Tarney in 1946.[11]

The Lancashire Record Office has a number of items relating to the firm. Firstly there are plans, drawings and correspondence relating to churches whose records are now lodged at the Record Office. In addition there are two books which relate to the final twenty years of the firm and give us a unique insight into the work done by Harry Paley. These are a Specification Book of 1925–39 for Austin and Paley and their Account Book of 1927–42. Both survived the destruction of the office records and provide us with a wealth of information about work at the office from 1924 until the final closure of the firm. It is a great pity that similar records do not exist for the previous seventy five years, for these books which provide details of contract prices and the contractors, if duplicated for an earlier era, would make the study of the firm much more comprehensive.

One example where more complete records survive is at Barrow. Here the Record Office contains the first two Building Registers for the town. These Registers detail the applications by builders for the erection of new buildings and include the name of the architect involved if there was one. Using this source we can list the buildings Paley and Austin were involved with from 1873 to the end of the century but not those done by Paley or Sharpe earlier. It is not always possible to tell whether, having applied to erect a building, this was actually done. The Barrow evidence however shows Paley and Austin to have been particularly active in the 1870s and 1880s as the town grew rapidly; but the slowing of this growth seems to equate with the closure of their Barrow Office in the 1890s. There did however continue to be a trickle of commissions from Barrow and district into the early part of the century.

Finally no discussion of the sources which exist for the construction of a list of their works would be complete without mention of the work of David McLoughlin. As the result of many years study he has an unrivalled knowledge, both of the buildings themselves and of the location of their records. His work has enabled us to track down and identify buildings not described elsewhere.

If the impression given by this summary of the available sources is that it is full and comprehensive, then this is wrong. All too often one source replicates information from another and we have little or no information for a large part of their output. Collectively, however, the sources listed do enable us to construct a tentative list of their major works, but we cannot assume that it is a wholly reliable and completely comprehensive list of all their works.

Any study of the work done by an architect during the course of his professional career throws up a number of questions (something especially true of those working in the nineteenth century).

There are two major questions which can be posed about the work either of an individual architect or a long running practice. Firstly, how much work did they do and thus what was their total output of designs and commissions? (This should include commissions that were never built, in order to be comprehensive.) Secondly, and the more difficult question to answer, what was the scale of each design? All practices had a range of types of work they were involved in, often several jobs being on-going at the same time. Such work could range in size and scale from the design and subsequent oversight of the erection of a complete church or mansion, through the restoration or renovation of a church, to small scale alterations and renovations. In many cases it is the details of these smaller commissions which are missing from the lists of work of architects but which are necessary to get an overall picture of the work of a practice. Such work ranges from a memorial window, new fixtures like reredos, pulpit or a set of pews, to a new wing on a house or a new chancel for a church. The three books of designs in Lancaster Library give details of a large number of such small works, especially fixtures designed to be added to buildings designed by other architects. Undoubtedly some of the smaller jobs were designed by members of the office other than the partners, including quite possibly some of their articled pupils.

It is obvious that, even with the problems relating to source materials, we now possess a fairly complete list of the major works of the four Lancaster men. What we still lack, however, is a comprehensive list of their minor work. For example, we do not know all of the churches that Austin 'restored and made additions to' nor, with the odd exception, the numerous schools that Paley designed. It is here that our list is most complete for the period 1925–42, as for this period we can use the firm's Specification Book in the Lancashire Record Office to compile a comprehensive list of Harry Paley's work.

In the absence of the firm's records the creation of a definitive list of ALL the work they undertook is, I feel, an impossibility. Given the limited nature of the various source materials, its construction would be a lifetime's endeavour and even then would be likely to contain errors, if only of omission.

The list that is used for the subsequent analysis of their work is the best that exists on the basis of present day information. This is not to say that it will not continue to be updated in the light of ongoing research. As it stands, it contains the vast majority of their major works, though there may still be some work wrongly attributed and some commissions which were never executed, for example Christ's Hospital, Horsham. Thus the list which has been utilised for analysis in the rest of this chapter is dated 1997 and is as complete a record of their work as is practicable. When additions were made to a building of theirs or when it is one of a group of buildings they designed, then the various commissions are treated together. Where minor works were undertaken they are listed, but they are usually less detailed for the period 1851–1925.

Table VI
List of known works, 1836–1942

	Major	*Restorations**	*Minor*	*Total*
Sharpe 1836–45	35	2	4	41
Sharpe and Paley 1846–51	15	8	0	23
Paley 1851–67	66	26	5	97
Paley and Austin 1868–86	142	55	11	208
Paley, Austin and Paley 1886–95	28	11	4	43
Austin and Paley 1895–1914	52	24	5	81
Austin, Paley and Austin 1914–16	1	2	1	4
H A Paley 1916–42	31	20	88	139
TOTAL	370	148	118	636

* includes alterations and additions chiefly to churches.

One particular area of work that is poorly represented in the list of minor works is that of fixtures and ornaments. The books of drawings (on tracing paper) in Lancaster Library chiefly relate to church fixtures and fittings like pulpits or pews. In most cases they are not dated unless they are part of a complete church commission and some are very small jobs, designed as 'one-offs' for an existing church; some have no attribution at all.

What then of the output of the practice from 1836–1942?

As can be seen from Table VI, the century that the firm was in existence saw the design and erection of a large number of buildings

48 St Michael and All Angel's Church, Howe Bridge, Atherton, 1875–77, by Paley and Austin.

along with restoration work and a large number of minor works. The present state of our knowledge suggests that they undertook around 600 commissions which range widely in scale and location. Graph 1 shows this output by decade from 1836–1942. Initially the output shows a slow start with Sharpe working alone until he takes Paley on as a

49 Holy Trinity, Millom, 1874–7, by Paley and Austin.

GRAPH 2
New Chapel & Church Commissions,
(by decade)

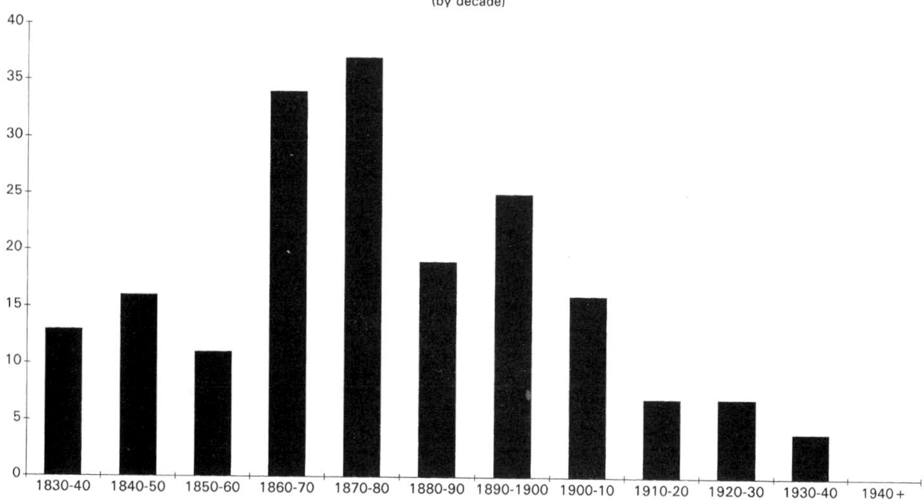

large houses, for example Holker Hall and Thurland Castle. A second is industry (especially railways) and commerce, for example Paley and Austin were the official architects for the Lancaster and Skerton Co-operative Society and both E. G. Paley and H. J. Austin worked for the Furness Railway, designing stations from Grange to Foxfield as well as works in Barrow (see Appendix B). Paley also designed the Lancaster Waggon Works in 1864–5. A third category is public buildings. There were several large commissions for hospitals including the Royal Albert, The Royal Lancaster Infirmary and the North Lonsdale Hospital, Barrow, while earlier Sharpe had been involved in extending the County Mental Hospital (on the Moor) in Lancaster. Large amounts of school work was undertaken including work at public schools like Sedbergh, Giggleswick, St Bees and Rossall.

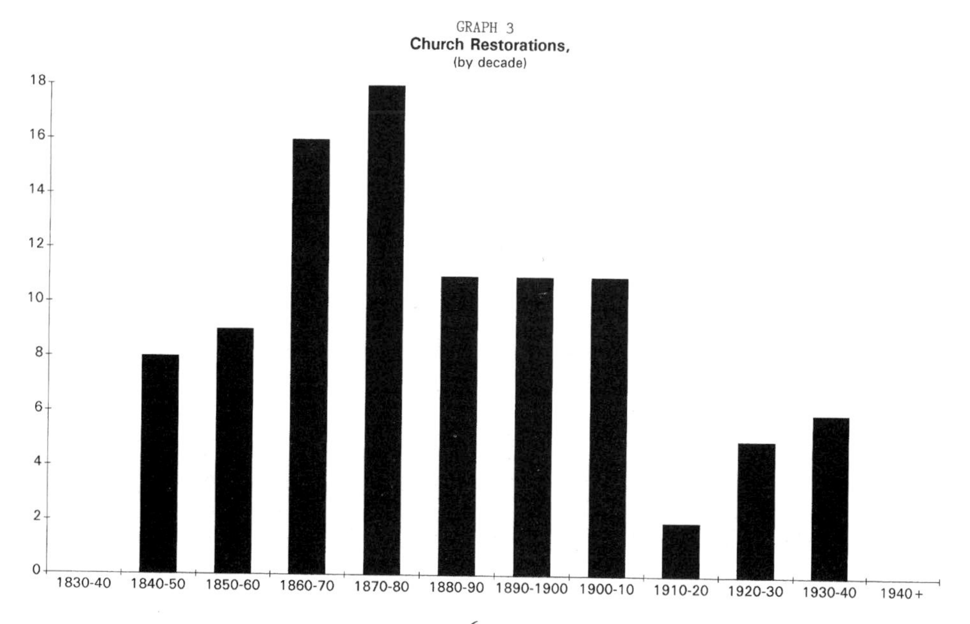

GRAPH 3
Church Restorations,
(by decade)

GRAPH 4

Non-Ecclesiastical Commissions,
(by decade)

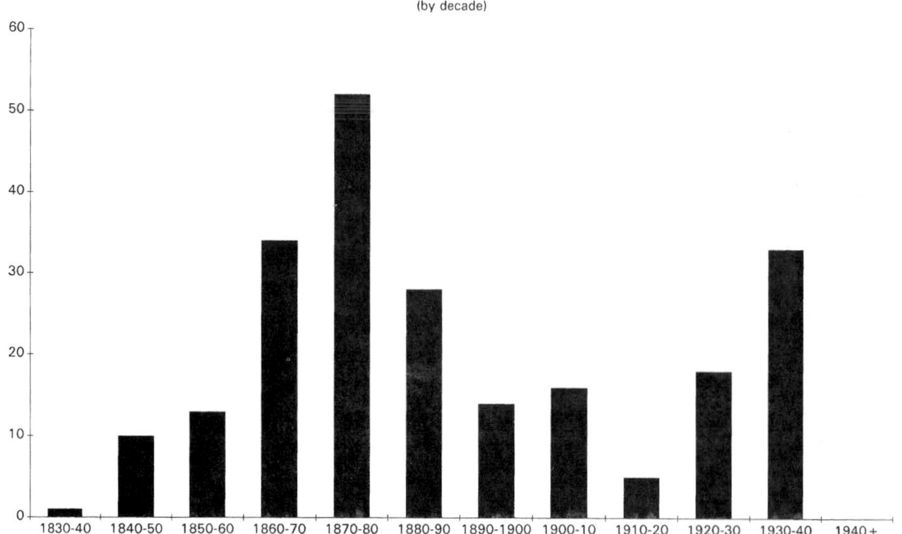

Unfortunately we know far less about their work on schools built for the various local education authorities in what is today Lancashire and Cumbria.

As graph 4 shows, this category of work peaks in the 1870s and 1880s and thereafter declines, especially industry and commerce, for example there is no more railway work once they close their Barrow office. Is this decline due to a conscious decision to concentrate more exclusively upon ecclesiastical work or because the range of work they had done before was no longer available? The period 1890–1900 shows a particularly marked decline but this may be due to the incomplete nature of the data available. They did continue some non-church work until the end, especially schools and hospitals, and almost the last major work of Harry Paley was the Nurses Home for the Royal Lancaster Infirmary. He was adding to this hospital right up to the Second World War and the last job I have evidence for, is the design for a 'degassing unit' there in 1942. This does not, however, ever seem to have been built! The adding of new buildings or smaller additions to works that they had originally designed is a feature of the practice and valued long-standing clients continued to commission new work, a credit both to the firm's reputation and the quality of their design. The Royal Albert Hospital, Lancaster which was built to the designs of E. G. Paley in 1868–70, though the central tower was the work of H. J. Austin, had additions made to it designed by the firm into this century, including the Ashton Wing in 1901.

Maps 1–9 have been constructed to show the distribution of the works of the practice from its very earliest days to its closure in 1942. A study of these maps shows that their work can be classified as being located at one of three scales – local, regional and national. Initially there is a strong local influence which begins with Sharpe but continues throughout the life of the firm. A good deal of work was thus done in Lancaster, Morecambe and in the nearby Lune valley settlements. Even from his earliest days however Sharpe sought work further afield and he obtained a number of commissions in the Blackburn area. It was this early work that probably led to further commissions in central Lancashire. In addition however, he must have made a number of contacts through his marriage in 1843 to Elizabeth Fletcher of the

Hollins, Bolton. Her father Colonel John Fletcher had discovered deposits of fireclay at his Ladyshore Colliery at Little Lever and his son conceived the idea of building the newly promoted church there in terra cotta. The commission for St Stephen's Church and All Martyrs at Lever Bridge, the earliest of his 'Pot Churches' had been given to Sharpe by his future brother-in-law in 1842. The regional aspect of the work of the practice continued throughout the time Paley worked alone. As Map 5 shows at the peak of the practice's fortunes, Paley and Austin carried out a large number of commissions in the North West as well as some in Yorkshire and North Eastern England. By this time the practice could be said to have a North Country wide reputation and spread of work, rather than being seen solely as a Lancashire firm. It is notable that up to the closure of their office in Barrow, the Furness area produced the location for a large number of commissions.

On a national scale the picture is far more limited. Admittedly they did work outside the North and in fact two of Harry Paley's last works were in Coventry. However on the scale at which they operated outside the North of England they cannot be compared with those 'national practices' located in London. Map 1 shows the location of all of their works including counties other than Lancashire. If we remove the buildings designed for the nearby counties of Westmorland, Cumberland, Cheshire and West Yorkshire and include those works of 'unknown location' less than a third of their output is outside the North.

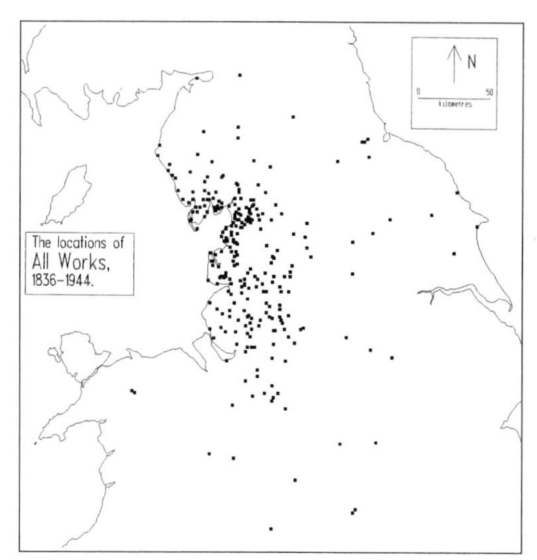

Map 1.

Even if they were not seen as national figures in their profession, they were nonetheless recognised nationally by their peers. Sharpe was a Gold Medallist of the RIBA on the basis of his historical writings, Paley was

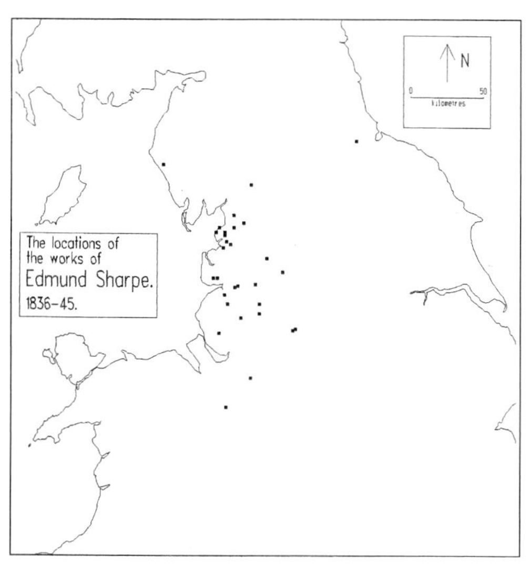

Map 2.

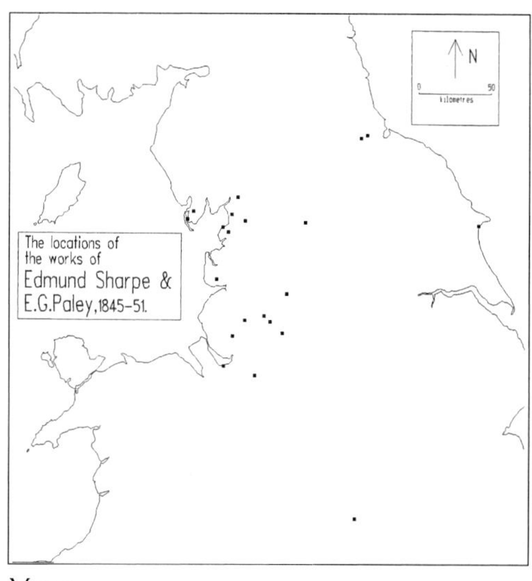

Map 3.

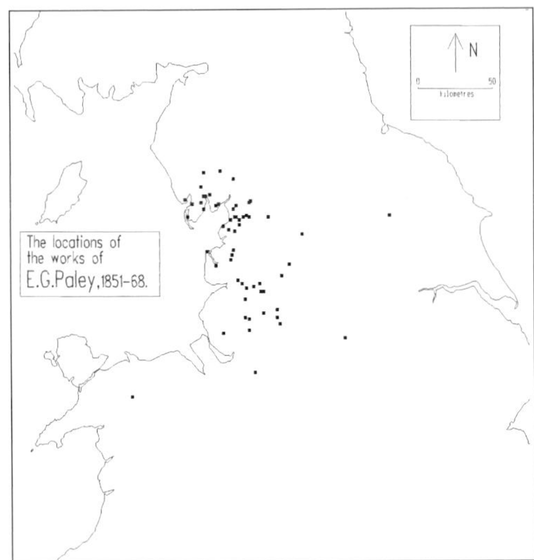

Map 4.

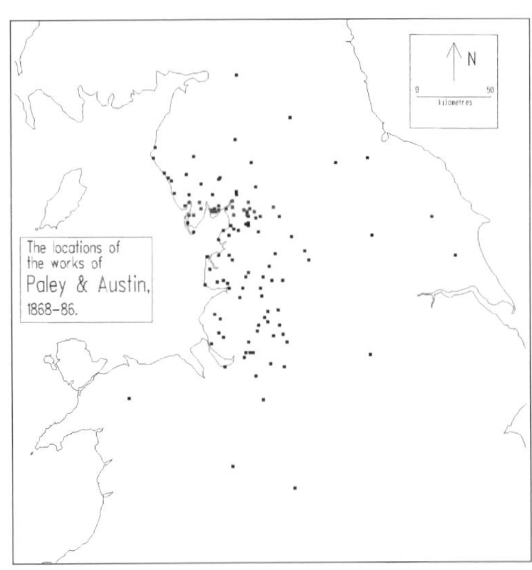

Map 5.

a FRIBA and a member of the Institute's Committee, while Austin had a national reputation specifically in the field of church restoration. Their reputation certainly extended outside the North West, even if their works were not spread as widely as there. They were essentially a regional practice, albeit a major one, with a sphere of influence and reputation chiefly in the North, with work in Cumbria, Yorkshire, Durham as well as Lancashire. This regional quality is something they have in common with other practices like Lockwood and Mawson, Douglas and Gardner, Austin and Johnson, Weightman and Hadfield, all of whom were working in the last century in the provinces. The difference between such firms and Paley and Austin may be to do with scale and importance. What we have in Lancaster is a major practice which for a time may have been by repute and output the leading practice in the north, a view supported by Pevsner who said that they were the 'best firm of Gothicists in the north of England'.[14]

The final part of this chapter provides a more detailed description of the work of the practice in its heyday. It takes the period 1851–1895 during which time first Paley and later Paley and Austin were in practice. The work which dates from this period is then analysed in terms of its overall range and output as well as ecclesiastical work.

Map 4 shows the output of Edward Paley between 1851–1868 when he worked alone as an architect. Following a relatively slow start as he sought to establish himself, his commissions grew apace so that by the 1860s he had a thriving practice. At this time he was averaging five or six commissions per year. At present we know of ninety seven commissions (five without dates) but other work at a variety of scales almost certainly needs adding. In some cases the work was an addition to an earlier commission or an additional building to add to an assemblage of buildings. Thus in addition to building St Peter's Church, Lancaster itself (1857–9), he was also involved in designing for it a presbytery, a convent and an adjacent church School. The major part of his output was ecclesiastical, with thirty three new churches, and additions/alterations to another twenty six – in all sixty one per cent of his work. Work on houses and schools make up another twenty eight per cent.

It is the remaining eleven per cent of his work which gives lie to the idea that he was just a church architect and also provides a fascinating insight into the work of a Victorian architect. Here there is a market

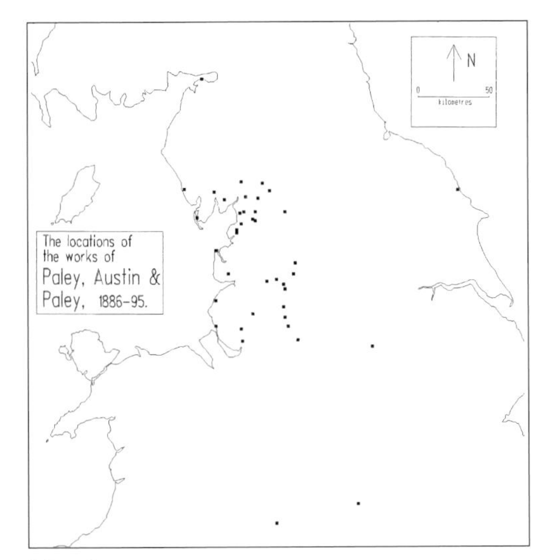

Map 6.

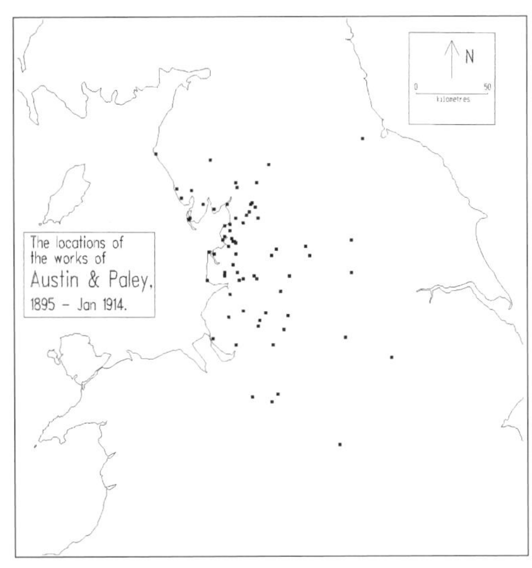

Map 7.

(Barrow), two railway stations and two hotels, a war memorial (to the Crimean War) and the Royal Albert Hospital. The most interesting commission is that for the Lancaster Waggon Works[15] which still stands on the Caton Road minus its chimney and is a fine stone built structure, notable for its fine clock tower and office block.

An analysis of his work by location (there were eighty nine locations) shows that the largest percentage of his work (thirty per cent) was in north Lancashire which is defined as the present day Lancaster District with another seventeen per cent from the Furness area including Barrow. If we add to this forty-four per cent from the rest of Lancashire (pre-1974 boundaries) and what was formerly Cumberland and Westmorland then it is obvious that Paley was pre-eminently a north west architect. Only nine per cent of his work derives from the areas outside the North West with for example churches in Bradford and Rylestone, a Clapham school and restoration work on churches at Crayke and Easingwold (where his father had been the Vicar).

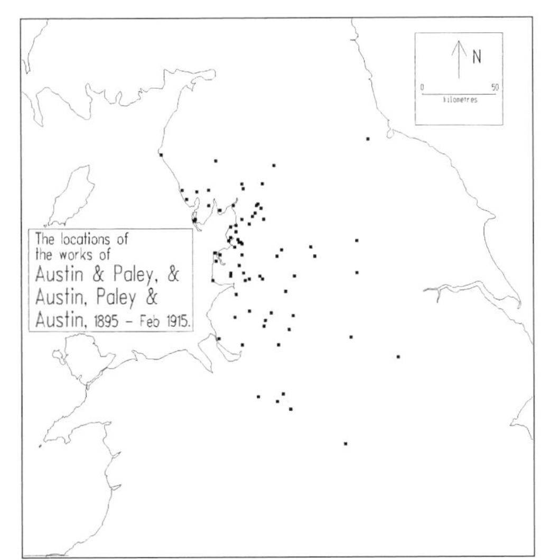

Map 8.

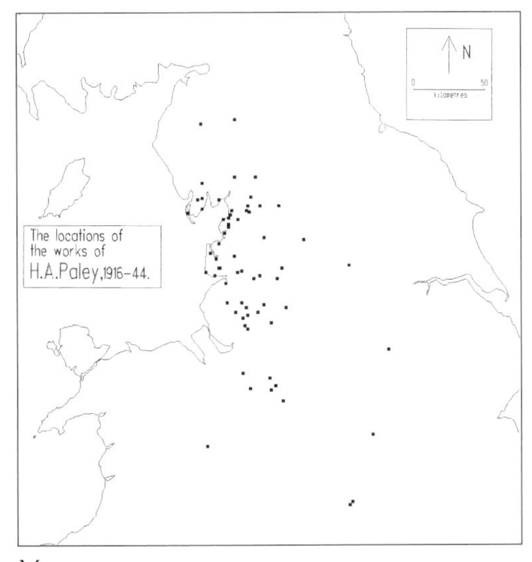

Map 9.

A comparison of the work of Edward Paley with that of the work of Paley and Austin (with Harry Paley as a partner from 1886) identifies both similarities and differences between the two periods. (NB the total for the period 1868–1895 includes the figure for the last seven years when the firm went under the name of Paley, Austin and Paley).

Firstly there is the scale of output. The two men (and later three) over a period of twenty seven years had two hundred and fifty one commissions compared with the ninety seven of Paley in seventeen years. There was an increased annual output, with an average of nearly ten commissions per year. Again the largest single category of work was ecclesiastical with fifty nine per cent for new churches and restorations etc. A further twenty-five per cent is houses and schools while the remaining fifteen per cent is made up of a range of commissions. These include a number of surprises. Thus Paley designed a bridge at Caton and at this time, they did shipyard work in Barrow. In Lancaster they did the decorative top to a chimney for Messrs Storey Brothers, the Storey Institute in Lancaster, three banks and two hospitals, as well as restoring Dalton Castle at Dalton in Furness.

After noting the difference in the amount of work done, the result of two or three architects rather than one man working alone, the major difference between the two periods is to do with the location of their designs. Now north Lancashire and Furness amount for twenty-nine per cent of commissions (Paley forty-seven per cent) while the rest of Lancashire with thirty one per cent is again less than the thirty seven per cent of Paley. The big difference is the increase in work coming from areas outside Lancashire. This has doubled, with work in Cheshire, Staffordshire and the West Riding (see Maps 3 and 4).

It is during the period when Paley and Austin worked together that the practice had a reputation and sphere of influence that extended throughout the northern half of England with commissions coming from an area extending from the Midlands to Scotland. Much still remains to be discovered about how they obtained many of these commissions but it must in part be the result of their growing reputation which resulted from their earlier works. During this time it is easy to see why the reputation of 'Paley and Austin' stood so high among Victorian architects and why their semi-national reputation, once created, lasted into the early part of this century, and has left a legacy of superbly designed buildings throughout the north of England.

Footnotes

1 J. Fawcett (ed.), *Seven Victorian Architects*, Thames and Hudson, 1976.

2 D. Cole, *The work of Sir Gilbert Scott*, Architectural Press, 1980.

3 E.g. that of H. J. Austin in *The Builder*, April 2 1915.

4 *Lancaster Guardian*, 12 May 1877.

5 Source unknown. Lancaster Biographies Scrapbook, Lancaster Library.

6 *Lancaster Observer*, 25 Jan. 1895.

7 *Lancaster Guardian*, 26 Jan. 1895.

8 *Lancaster Guardian*, 27 March 1915.

9 *Lancaster Observer*, 26 March 1915.

10 Mr G. M. Leather has a small collection of their drawings and plans including some for the work at the Ripley Hospital.

11 A letter from Mr Tarney to Mr D. Anderson in 1948 confirms that the plans and drawing books of the practice were sent to salvage and that a selection of the firm's work was sent by request to the Royal Institute of British Architects.

12 N. Pevsner, *The Buildings of North Lancashire*, p. 33.

13 N. Pevsner, *The Buildings of Cheshire*, p. 36.

14 N. Pevsner, *Some Architectural Writers of the Nineteenth Century*, *op cit*, 1972.

15 Paley had been a Director of the Lancaster Waggon Company.

Appendix A

The Buildings of Sharpe, Paley and Austin, 1836–1944

(Revised October 1996)

The Works of Edmund Sharpe, 1836–45

1/01	Bamber Bridge St Saviour New Church Romanesque style	Cuerden, Lancashire 1836–7	Major
1/02	Bamber Bridge New School? (authority is Jolley) Has a Lombardy frieze	Cuerden, Lancashire 1839–40	Major
1/03	Bickerton Holy Trinity New Church 13th Century Lancet style	Malpas, Cheshire 1839–40	Major
1/04	Blackburn Holy Trinity 1. New Church (Geometric style)	Lancs 1837–46	Major
	2. Sunday Schools	1843	Major
1/05	Blackburn St Mark New Church Romanesque style	Witton, Blackburn 1836–38	Major
1/06	Bretherton St John the Baptist New Church Pre Archaeological Perpendicular	Lancashire 1839–40	Major
1/07	Briercliffe St James New Church Gothic 13th century–15th century	Haggate, Harle Sykes, Burnley 1840–41	Major
1/08	Capenwray Hall New Mansion Perpendicular style	Capenwray, Nr Carnforth, N. Lancs 1844+	Major
1/09	Calder Bridge St Bridget New Church pre Archaeological Gothic/ Early English	Calder Bridge, Cumberland, Cumbria 1840–41/2?	Major
1/10	Chatburn Christ Church New Church Romanesque style	Clitheroe, Lancs 1838	Major
1/11	Cockerham	Cockerham, Lancs	Major

	Vicarage (Source is Stansfield)	1843?	
1/12	Dukinfield St John the Evangelist New Church Lancet/Early English style ... Pre Archaeological Gothic	Cheshire 1838?–41	Major
1/13	Farington St Paul New Church Pre-Archaeological including Romanesque	Preston, N. Lancs 1839–40	Major
1/14	Farington St Paul Parsonage (Stansfield is source)	Preston, N. Lancs 1839	Major
1/15	Howgill Holy Trinity New Church Lancet style	Sedbergh W (now N. Yorks) 1837–8	Major
1/16	Heysham Heysham Tower Large house extended and altered (tower added)	Heysham, Lancs 1836	Major
1/17	Kirkham St Michael New spire in Decorated style	Kirkham, Fylde, Lancs 1843–4	Major
1/18	Knowsley St Mary the Virgin New Church Lancet style	Nr Prescot, S. Lancs 1843–4	Major
1/19	Lancaster Grand Theatre Conversion of Theatre to Music Hall	N. Lancs 1843	Minor
1/20	Lancaster Castle New Cells (and Courts?)	N. Lancs 1836+	Minor
1/21	Lancaster Moor Hospital (Co. Lunatic Asylum) i. Chapel ii. Rear wings, large additions (with Paley)	N. Lancs 1842 1840s	 Major Major
1/22	Lancaster St Thomas New Church Pre-Archaeological Lancet style	N. Lancs 1839–40	Major
1/23	Lancaster (Middle St) Bluecoat School	N. Lancs 1849–50	Major
1/24	Lancaster Priory Church internal alterations; roof	N. Lancs 1848–9	Minor
1/25	Lancaster The Higher Greaves	N. Lancs	Minor

	alterations to a private house	c1865	
1/26	Lancaster Masonic Hall	N. Lancs no date	Minor
1/27	Lever Bridge St Stephen & All Martyrs New Church Decorated style	Bolton, Lancs 1842–6	Major
1/28	Lever Bridge Vicarage	Bolton, Lancs 1844	Major
1/29	Maudsley St Peter New Church Gothic 13th Century - 15th Century	Ormskirk, Lancs 1840	Major
1/30	Morecambe Holy Trinity New Church Pre Archaeological Gothic of 13th Century - 15th Century	Morecambe, Lancs 1840–1	Major
1/31	Redmarshall 1. St Cuthbert – Restoration 2. Rectory (P Meadows communication)	Co. Durham 1845	Major
1/32	Scholes St Catherine New Church Pre Archaeological Gothic	Wigan, Lancs 1840–1	Major
1/33	Scotforth St Paul New Church Romanesque style	Scotforth, Lancaster 1874–6	Major
1/34	Stalybridge St George New Church Transitional style	Stalybridge, Cheshire 1838–40	Major
1/35	Walmsley Christ Church New Church Lancet style	Turton, Lancs 1839–40	Major
1/36	Winsford Christ Church New Church (demolished 1880)	Cheshire 1845	Major
1/37	Wray Holy Trinity New Church Pre Archaeological style/ Lancet	Wray, N. Lancs 1839–41	Major
1/38	Wyreside Hall New front	Dolphinholme, N. Lancs 1843–4	Major

Railways

1/39	Caton Railway Bridges	Caton, N. Lancs Crook O'Lune pre 1849	Major
1/40	Galgate	Galgate, N. Lancs	Major

	Skew Bridge	pre 1840	
1/41	Lancaster	Lancaster	Major
	Green Ayre Station	pre 1849	

The Works of Edmund Sharpe and E. G. Paley, 1845–51

It should be noted that it is likely that many of these works were probably carried out by Paley alone but I have no evidence to prove this.

2/01	Bacup Christ Church New Church Second Pointed/ Decorated style	Bacup, Lancs 1854	Major
2/02	Barrow St Mary, Walney Island New Church (demolished 1930)	Barrow-in-Furness, Lancs 1853	Major
2/03	Barrow Hotel converted from a disused manor house	Barrow-in-Furness, Lancs 1847	Major
2/04	Bishopton St Peter Rebuilding-nave chiefly Late 13th style	Bishopton, Co. Durham 1846–7	Major
2/05	Bridlington St Mary (Bridlington Priory) New roof	E. Yorks (N. Humberside) 1846–57	Major
2/06	Conistone St Mary Rebuilt chapel and remodelled church Romanesque style	Conistone, W. Yorks 1846	Major
2/07	Coventry St Thomas New Church Decorated style	Coventry, Warwicks 1848–9	Major
2/08	Dalton Dalton Castle Restoration and rebuilding	Dalton-in-Furness 1854	Minor
2/09	Davenham St Wilfred Church rebuilt in a Decorated (Geometric) style of the late 13th/early 14th Century	Davenham, Cheshire 1847	Major
2/10	Hornby Castle Remodelling inc. new facade	Hornby, Lancs 1849–52	Major
2/11	Ince Ince Hall Italianate style (now demolished)	Ince, Ellesmere Port, Cheshire 1849	Major
2/12	Lever Bridge St Stephen and All Martyrs Church School	Bolton, Lancs 1851	Major
2/13	Lancaster Savings Bank Remodelled in classical style	Lancaster, Lancs 1848	Major
2/14	Lancaster	Lancaster, Lancs	Major

	Militia Barracks (South Road) Baronial style	1854	
2/15	Lancaster Infant School on Moor Road	Lancaster, Lancs 1851	Major
2/16	Lancaster Grammar School Symmetrically gabled Gothic	Lancaster, Lancs 1851–2	Major
2/17	Lancaster House in Dallas Road	Lancaster, Lancs 1853	Major
2/18	Morecambe North Western Hotel (now demolished)	Morecambe, Lancs 1847	Major
2/19	Preston Patrick St Gregory Rebuilt in Perpendicular style	Westmorland (Cumbria) 1852–3	Major
2/20	Ringley St Saviour New Church Lancet/Early English style	Kearsley, Manchester 1851–4	Major
2/21	Rusholme Holy Trinity New Church Decorated style c1300	Platt, Manchester 1845–6	Major
2/22	Sutton St Nicholas New Church Early 14th Century style	St Helens, S. Lancs 1848–9	Major
2/23	Thorpe Thewles Holy Trinity New Church (Demolished 1866–7)	Thorpe Thewles, Co. Durham 1849	Major
2/24	Warton St Oswald Church Renovation work on South arcade	Warton, N. Lancs 1848–9	Minor
2/25	Wigan All Saints Rebuild of Parish Church Perpendicular style	Wigan, S. Lancs 1845–50	Major
2/26	Wrea Green St Nicholas 'Improved' (restored) in 13th Century plate/geometric style	Wrea Green, Fylde, Lancs 1848–9	Major

The Buildings of E. G. Paley

It should be noted that a full list of his own works would almost certainly include some done by "Sharpe and Paley". See the note at the start of Sharpe and Paley.

In addition there are probably works entered as designed by Paley and Austin which were designed by Paley alone.

3/01	Allithwaite St Mary	Allithwaite (Nr Grange) N. Lancs (now Cumbria)	Major

	New Church Decorated style	1864–5	
3/02	Allithwaite School and School House	Allithwaite (Nr Grange) N. Lancs (now Cumbria) 1865	Major
3/03	Allithwaite Vicarage} Coach House} N. B. All three were done as one commission.	Allithwaite (Nr Grange) N. Lancs (now Cumbria) 1865	Major
3/04	Aughton St Saviour New Church Lancet style	N. Lancs 1864	Major
3/05	Barrow-in-Furness St George New Church Geometrical/Decorated style	Barrow, N. Lancs, now Cumbria 1859–61	Major
3/06	Barrow-in-Furness St James New Church Decorated 13th Century style (N. B. The Austin influence in this spire)	Barrow, N. Lancs, now Cumbria 1867–9	Major
3/07	Barrow-in-Furness St James School	Barrow, N. Lancs now Cumbria 1867	Major
3/08	Barrow-in-Furness New Market Gothic style (Now demolished)	Barrow, N. Lancs now Cumbria 1866	Major
3/09	Barrow-in-Furness Abbotswood New Mansion Neo-gothic style (Now demolished)	Barrow, N. Lancs now Cumbria 1857	Major
3/10	Barrow-in-Furness Railway Station (on the Strand)	Barrow, N. Lancs now Cumbria 1862–3	Major
3/11	Barrow-in-Furness Furness Railway Offices	Barrow, N. Lancs now Cumbria 1862–3	Major
3/12	Barrow-in-Furness Furness Abbey Station	Barrow, N. Lancs now Cumbria 1865	Major
3/13	Barrow-in-Furness Furness Abbey Hotel Additions and alterations. Tudor style	Barrow, N. Lancs now Cumbria 1866–9	Major
3/14	Barrow-in-Furness Marine Villa/Piel Cottage Marine Villa/Piel Cottage - Billiard Room	Barrow, N. Lancs now Cumbria 1861 1865	Major
3/15	Bardsea School and School Master's House	Nr Barrow, N. Lancs now Cumbria no date	Major
3/16	Blackburn St Thomas New Church	Blackburn, Lancs 1864–5	Major

	Decorated/Geometrical style (Now demolished)		
3/17	Blackburn St Thomas Church School	Blackburn, Lancs 1864–5	Major
3/18	Blawith St John the Baptist New Church Decorated style	Blawith, N. Lancs now Cumbria 1860–66	Major
3/19	Bolton-le-Sands St Michael Restoration work/chancel?	Bolton-le-Sands, N. Lancs 1863–4	Minor
3/20	Bolton St Peter New Church Decorated style	Bolton, Lancs 1867–71	Major
3/21	Bolton-le-Moors St Matthew New Church Decorated Geometric style	Little Lever, Bolton-le-Moors, S. Lancs 1865	Major
3/22	Bonds St Mary & Michael RC 1. New Church 13th Century Decorated style 2. Presbytery	Garstang , N. Lancs 1857–8	Major
3/23	Bradford Holy Trinity (Leeds Road) New Church Late 13th Century Decorated style (Now demolished 1966)	Bradford, W. Yorks 1864–5	Major
3/24	Brindle St James (Chancel plus renovation)	Brindle, N. Lancs 1869–70	Major
3/25	Brookhouse St Paul (Rebuilt except for Tower) Perpendicular style	Caton, N. Lancs 1864–7	Major
3/26	Brookhouse Moorgarth (Additions to former workhouse to make it into a house)	Caton, N. Lancs 1869?	Minor
3/27	Browhead Hall	Windermere, Westmorland, now Cumbria 1869?	Major
3/28	Broughton-in-Furness Eccle Riggs (House) Tudor style	Broughton, N. Lancs now Cumbria 1865	Major
3/29	Burnley St Peter Restoration/new roof Perpendicular style	Burnley, N. Lancs 1854	Major
3/30	Bury Holy Trinity New Church Decorated style	Bury, S. Lancs 1864–5	Major
3/31	Burton-in-Kendal	Burton-in-Kendal	Major

	Additions to Dalton Hall Classical style (Now demolished)	Westmorland, now Cumbria 1859	
3/32	Capel Garmon St Garmon New Church	Llanwrst, Denbigh 1863	Major
3/33	Casterton Holy Trinity New Chancel	Westmorland, now Cumbria 1860?	Major
3/34	Chorley St Laurence Restoration work (virtually rebuilt)	Chorley, S. Lancs 1859–61	Major
3/35	Churchtown St Helen Restoration (ref Hewitson Northward)	Churchtown, N. Lancs 1864–9	Major
3/36	Clapham New C. of E. School	Clapham, W. Yorks now N. Yorks 1864	Major
3/37	Coniston Station 'Swiss Chalet style'	N. Lancs, now Cumbria 1862	Major
3/38	Colne St Bartholomew Restoration	Colne, N. Lancs 1856–7	Major
3/39	Crayke St Cuthbert Restoration & N. Aisle	Crayke, N. Yorks 1862–3	Minor
3/40	Darwen St John Turncroft New Church (Now demolished)	Darwen, N. Lancs 1864	Major
3/41	Davenham Lych Gate	Davenham, Cheshire 1860	Minor
3/42	Easingwold St John & All Saints Porch Restoration	Easingwold, N. Yorks 1853 1858	Major
3/43	Egton St Mary Rebuilt	Penny Bridge, Lancs now Cumbria 1864	Major
3/44	Grange over Sands Grange Hotel	Grange over Sands N. Lancs now Cumbria 1866	Major
3/45	Greenodd Station	N. Lancs now Cumbria 1869+	Major
3/46	Gressingham St John the Evangelist Restoration	Gressingham, N. Lancs 1862	Major
3/47	Haverthwaite Station	N. Lancs now Cumbria 1869+	Major
3/48	Hindley St Peter New Church Decorated style	Hindley, Wigan, S. Lancs 1866	Major
3/49	Hindley Schools and House?	Hindley, Wigan, S. Lancs 1861	Major
3/50	Hoddlesden	Hoddlesden, N. Lancs	Major

	St Paul New Church Decorated style 13th Century	1862–3	
3/51	Ince-in-Makerfield Christ Church New Church Decorated style	Ince-in-Makerfield, S. Lancs 1863–4	Major
3/52	(Over) Kellet St Cuthbert Restoration	Over-Kellet, N. Lancs 1863–4	Major
3/53	Kirkby Lonsdale St Mary Restoration (inc. South Porch)	Kirkby Lonsdale Westmorland, now Cumbria 1866	Major
3/54	Knowsley St Mary the Virgin added Transepts (Pulpit and Desk too in 1860)	Knowsley, S. Lancs 1860	Major
3/55	Lancaster St Mary (Priory) Restoration/Renewal Removal of Galleries } New W. organ Gallery } Pulpit moved; pews moved	Lancaster, Lancs 1856–8 1864	Major
3/56	Lancaster St Peter New RC Church Decorated (1300) style	Lancaster, Lancs 1857–9	Major
3/57	Lancaster St Peter Presbytery Convent School	Lancaster, Lancs 1859 1853 1851–2	Major
3/58	Lancaster The Royal Albert Hospital New Imbecile Asylum	Lancaster, Lancs 1868–73	Major
3/59	Lancaster Cemetery (Moor) Chapels} Gardeners House} Registrar's House}	Lancaster, Lancs 1854–5	Major
3/60	Lancaster Cemetery (Moor) Crimean War Memorial	Lancaster, Lancs 1860	Minor
3/61	Lancaster Grand Theatre Extended for Athenaeum Society	Lancaster, Lancs 1856	Minor
3/62	Lancaster St John's National School Cable Street (Now demolished)	Lancaster, Lancs 1868	Major
3/63	Lancaster Wagon and Carriage Works, Caton Road	Lancaster, Lancs 1864–5	Major
3/64	Lancaster St Michael on the Moor (in the Moor Hospital)	Lancaster, Lancs 1866	Major
3/65	Lancaster Congregational Sunday	Lancaster, Lancs 1855–6	Major

	School, Middle Street		
3/66	Lancaster The Greaves (private house)	Lancaster, Lancs c1855	Major
3/67	Lancaster Parkfield House Greaves Road New House	Lancaster, Lancs no date (pre 1872)	Major
3/68	Lancaster New House (at bottom of Bowerham Road)	Lancaster, Lancs no date	Major
3/69	Lancaster St Thomas New Spire	Lancaster, Lancs 1852–3	Major
3/70	Livesey St Andrew New Church	Livesey, Blackburn Lancs 1866–7	Major
3/71	Lowton St Mary New Church	Lowton, S. Lancs (Nr Wigan) 1860–1	Major
3/72	Melling St Wilfred Restoration	Melling, N. Lancs 1856–63?	Major
3/73	Morecambe Clark St Congregational New Church	Morecambe, N. Lancs 1863	Major
3/74	Newfield Hall	no location no date	Major
3/75	Penwortham St Mary Restoration (arches, nave, porch)	Penwortham, Preston 1855–6	Major
3/76	Preston St Mark New church Fourteenth Century style	Preston, Lancs 1862–6	Major
3/77	Preston St John the Divine Parish Church Tower groining Font	Preston, Lancs 1856	Minor
3/78	Preston All Saints New bell tower?	Preston, Lancs no date	Minor
3/79	Quernmore St Peter New Church Late 13th Century/early 14th Century Decorated style	Quernmore, N. Lancs 1859–60	Major
3/80	Rossall School Chapel: St John the Baptist	Rossall, Fleetwood, N. Lancs 1861	Major
3/81	Rossall Rossall School N. Range Domestic Building & Dining Room Pavillion	Rossall, Fleetwood, N. Lancs 1853 1859 1860	Major

	Swimming Pool?	1868	
3/82	Rossall Rossall School Gatehouse	Rossall, Fleetwood, N. Lancs 1867	Major
3/83	Rylstone St Peter New Church	Rylstone, W. Yorks 1853	Major
3/84	Scorton Wyresdale Hall Gothic style Enlarged	Scorton, N. Lancs 1856–58 1865	Major
3/85	Singleton St Anne New Church Early English style	Fylde, N. Lancs 1860–1	Major
3/86	Singleton Singleton School	Fylde, N. Lancs 1862	Major
3/87	Thwaites St Anne New Church Decorated/Geometric style	Thwaites, Nr Millom Cumberland, now Cumbria 1854	Major
3/88	Ulverston St Mary Considerable rebuilding (Later work possibly Paley and Austin pre 1885 and 1905)	Ulverston, Lancs, now Cumbria 1864–66	Major
3/89	Walton le Dale All Saints New Church Pre-Archaeological plan but late 13th Century style	Higher Walton, Walton le Dale, Preston 1861–2	Major
3/90	Walton le Dale Vicarage	Higher Walton, Walton le Dale, Preston no date	Major
3/91	Wennington Wennington Hall Gothic style	Wennington, N. Lancs 1855–6	Major
3/92	Whitefield St Saviour Rebuilt church	Whitefield, near Radcliffe S. Lancs 1851	Major
3/93	Wigan All Saints Tower heightened	Wigan 1861	Minor
3/94	Wigan St James New Church Decorated style	Poolstock, Wigan 1863–6	Major
3/95	Woodlands St John the Evangelist New Church	Kirkby Ireleth, N. Lancs now Cumbria 1864–5	Major
3/96	Wrightington St James New Church Early English style	Wrightington, Chorley, Lancs 1857	Major
3/97	Yealand Conyers St Mary RC New Church Geometric style	Yealand Conyers, N. Lancs 1852	Major

The Works of Paley and Austin, 1868–1886

It must be remembered that even though the two men worked as a partnership they probably individually designed buildings. For example some would hold that Austin designed many of the churches and Paley did much of the other work. In addition the sketches that remain (and plans) sometimes have one or other names on them rather than both.

4/01	Alderley St Mary Restoration Perpendicular style	Nether Alderley, Macclesfield, Cheshire 1877–8	Major
4/02	Allithwaite Kents Bank Station	Allithwaite, N. Lancs now Cumbria 1865	Major
4/03	Altham St James Rebuilt chapel	Altham, Burnley, Lancs 1881	Major
4/04	Arnside Vicarage	Arnside, N. Lancs 1881	Major
4/05	Ashford Christ Church New Church Middle pointed style	Ashford, Kent 1865–7	Major
4/06	Atherton St John the Baptist Tower Extended Decorated/Perpendicular style	Atherton, S. Lancs 1878–80 1892–7 1887	Major
4/07	Atherton St Michael New Church	Howe Bridge, Atherton Lancs 1875–7	Major
4/08	Askham-in-Furness Station	Askam-in-Furness, Lancs now Cumbria 1877	Major
4/09	Barrow-in-Furness Presbyterian Church	Barrow, Lancs, Nr Cumbria 1874–5	Major
4/10	Barrow-in-Furness 4 temporary churches (Consecrated 1879) St Mark Rawlinson Street	Barrow, Lancs, Nr Cumbria 1877–8	Major
4/11	St Luke Salthouse Road		
4/12	St Matthew Highfield Road		
4/13	St John Island Road (Nov 17 1877) (All bar St Johns had vicarages designed by Paley and Austin in 1877)		
4/14	Barrow-in-Furness Shipworks (for Ashburner)	Barrow, Lancs, Nr Cumbria 1871–2	Major
4/15	Barrow-in-Furness Bank (Lancaster Banking Co.) Ramsden Square	Barrow, Lancs, Nr Cumbria 1873–4	Major
4/16	Barrow-in-Furness Bank	Barrow, Lancs, Nr Cumbria 1873	Major

	(Cumberland Union Banking Co.) Ramsden Square		
4/17	Barrow-in-Furness Cambridge St Schools Salthouse (additions 1880?)	Barrow, Lancs, Nr Cumbria 1875	Major
4/18	Barrow-in-Furness Jute Mill	Barrow, Lancs, Nr Cumbria 1870–71	Major
4/19	Barrow-in-Furness St George 'additions'	Barrow, Lancs, Nr Cumbria 1883	Minor
4/20	Barrow-in-Furness Town Hall design (not built)	Barrow, Lancs, Nr Cumbria 1877	Major
4/21	Barrow-in-Furness Masonic Hall (Abbey Road)	Barrow, Lancs, Nr Cumbria 1884	Major
4/22	Barrow-in-Furness St James: Vicarage	Barrow, Lancs, Nr Cumbria 1883	Major
4/23	Barrow-in-Furness Tenement Blocks: 1. Steamer St.} Barque St. Brig St} Schooner St. Ship St} 2. Michaelson Rd, Sloop St	Barrow, Lancs, Nr Cumbria 1881–4 1872–5	Major
4/24	Barrow-in-Furness Cavendish Park Villas	Barrow, Lancs, Nr Cumbria 1872	Major
4/25	Barrow-in-Furness North Lonsdale Hospital	Barrow, Lancs, Nr Cumbria 1883–7	Major
4/26	Barrow-in-Furness Piel Castle Restoration – turret & staircase for Duke of Buccleuch	Piel Island, Barrow, Lancs, Nr Cumbria 1876–8	Major
4/27	Barrow-in-Furness Piel Island Pilot Cottages	Piel Island, Barrow, Lancs, Nr Cumbria 1875	Major
4/28	Barrow-in-Furness Royalty Theatre (Star Music Hall) N. B. Was it ever built?	Barrow, Lancs, Nr Cumbria 1871	Major
4/29	Barrow-in-Furness Ramsden Dock Hydraulic Engine House	Barrow, Lancs, Nr Cumbria 1877	Major
4/30	Barrow-in-Furness Ramsden Dock Station & new warehouse	Barrow, Lancs, Nr Cumbria 1882	Major
4/31	Barrow-in-Furness Coffee Hotel on Barrow Island	Barrow, Lancs, Nr Cumbria 1882	Major
4/32	Barrow-in-Furness Alterations to Baths (Abbey Rd)	Barrow, Lancs, Nr Cumbria 1878	Minor
4/33	Barrow-in-Furness Central Station	Barrow, Lancs, Nr Cumbria 1882	Major
4/34	Beetham St Michael	Beetham, Westmorland Cumbria	Major

	Restoration inc porch	1872–4	
4/35	Beswick St Mary New Church (Demolished 1966)	Manchester 1877–8	Major
4/36	Bettws-y-Coed St Mary the Virgin New Church Norman transitional style	Caernarvonshire 1870	Major
4/37	Blackburn St Mark (Witton) Restoration & enlargement (N. transept and vestry) Romanesque style	Blackburn, Lancs 1881–7	Major
4/38	Bolton (Astley Bridge) All Souls New Church Decorated style	Bolton, Lancs 1879–81	Major
4/39	Bolton Astley Bridge School	Bolton, Lancs 1880–1	Major
4/40	Bolton St Saviour New Church Decorated style (Demolished 1975) Source – I. Nairn	Bolton, Lancs –1882	Major
4/41	Bolton (Halliwell) St Thomas New Church Early English style	Bolton, Lancs –1875	Major
4/42	Bolton Halliwell Lodge 'some work'	Bolton, Lancs no date	Minor
4/43	Bolton-le-Sands Holy Trinity/St Michael Restoration esp Nave	Bolton-le-Sands, N. Lancs 1880	Major
4/44	Bolton-by-Bowland School (added to 1906 - Stansfield)	W. Yorks 1874	Major
4/45	Bolton-by-Bowland School House?	W. Yorks no date	Major
4/46	Bootle Station	Cumberland, now Cumbria 1873	Major
4/47	Bowness St Martin Restoration	Windermere, Westmorland now Cumbria 1870–73	Major
4/48	Bradshaw St Maxentius Nave rebuilt (Tower retained) Early English style	North of Bolton, Lancs 1872	Major
4/49	Broughton St James New Church	Broughton, Salford (Manchester) 1877–9	Major
4/50	Broughton-in-Furness	Cumbria (was Lancs)	Major

	St Mary Magdalene Restoration (Chancel, Nave, new Aisle)	1874	
4/51	Broughton-in-Furness Foxfield Station	Cumbria (was Lancs) 1879	Major
4/52	Burnage St Margaret New Church Decorated style of 1300	Burnage, Manchester 1874–5	Major
4/53	Burnley St James New steeple and other changes	Burnley, Lancs 1869	Major
4/54	Burton-in-Lonsdale All Saints Church New Church	W. (now N.) Yorks. 1868–76	Major
4/55	Burton-in-Lonsdale Vicarage	W. (now N.) Yorks. no date	Major
4/56	Caton Road Bridge over the Lune (E. G. Paley, Bridgemaster for N. Lonsdale)	Caton, N. Lancs 1881–3	Major
4/57	Cark Station	N. Lancs (now Cumbria) 1875	Major
4/58	Cartmel St Mary & St Michael Priory. Restoration inc. Cavendish tomb	N. Lancs (now Cumbria) 1881?	Minor
4/59	Cheetham St John the Evangelist New Church	Cheetham, Manchester 1869–71	Major
4/60	Crewe St Barnabas New Church Perpendicular style	Crewe, Cheshire 1885–6	Major
4/61	Crewe St Barnabas Vicarage	Crewe, Cheshire no date	Major
4/62	Crewe School	Crewe, Cheshire 1887	Major
4/63	Crosscrake St Thomas New Church Geometric Decorated style	Westmorland, Cumbria 1875	Major
4/64	Clitheroe St Mary Magdalene Restoration	Clitheroe, N. Lancs 1881	Major
4/65	Clifton Lund Church (St John) New Tower	Clifton, (Newton with Lund) Nr Lytham 1874	Major
4/66	Daisy Hill St James New Church 12th Century – 13th Century style with Perpendicular windows	Daisy Hill, Bolton 1879–81	Major
4/67	Dalton-in-Furness St Mary	Dalton, N. Lancs (now Cumbria) 1883–5	Major

	New Church Free Decorated style		
4/68	Daresbury All Saints New Church Perpendicular style	Daresbury, Cheshire 1870–2	Major
4/69	Dale Ghyll New House Demolished (information from Michael Bottom-ley)	Hawcoat, Barrow in Furness no date	Major
4/70	Darwen St Cuthbert New Church	Darwen, Lancs 1874–8	Major
4/71	Darwen St Barnabas New Church	Darwen, Lancs 1884	Major
4/72	Davenham St Wilfred Chancel/Transepts	Davenham, Lancs 1870	Major
4/73	Dunningwell Mansion (information from Michael Bottomley)	Millom, Cumberland near Cumbria 1875	Major
4/74	Drigg Station	Cumberland, now Cumbria no date	Major
4/75	Eskdale (Boot) St Catherine Church restoration	Boot, Cumberland, now Cumbria 1881	Major
4/76	Fawley St Mary Restoration & Enlargement	Nr Henley-on-Thames 1882–3	Major
4/77	Fawley Fawley Court 'New wing and terraces'	Nr Henley-on-Thames no date	Major
4/78	Farnworth St John the Evangelist Chancel	Kearsley, Farnworth, Lancs 1871	Major
4/79	Finsthwaite St Peter New Church Norman style	N. Lancs, now Cumbria 1873–4	Major
4/80	Fleetwood St Peter East end remodelled	Fleetwood, Lancs 1880–3	Major
4/81	Garstang St Thomas the Apostle New Chancel	Garstang, N. Lancs 1876–80	Major
4/82	Goosnargh St Mary Nave rebuilt	Goosnargh, N. Lancs 1868–9	Major
4/83	Grappenhall St Wilfred Restoration	Grappenhall, Cheshire 1874	Major
4/84	Great Harwood St Bartholomew New Chancel	Great Harwood, Lancs 1886	Major

4/85	Grange-over-Sands Station rebuilt	Grange, Lancs, now Cumbria 1872	Major
4/86	Greenock St John the Evangelist New Church	Greenock, Renfrew, Nr Glasgow 1878	Major
4/87	Grimsargh St Michael New Church Decorated style	Grimsargh, N. Lancs 1868–71	Major
4/88	Giggleswick Giggleswick School Boarding House	Giggleswick, Nr Settle W. now N. Yorks 1867–9	Major
4/89	Halsall St Cuthbert Rebuilt Decorated style	Halsall, N. Lancs 1873; 1886	Major
4/90	Halton St Wilfred New Church Decorated style	Halton, N. Lancs 1876–7	Major
4/91	Hampsfield New Hall (Hampsfield Grange?)	N. Lancs, Cumbria? 1879	Major
4/92	Heversham now Cumbria Parish Church	Heversham, Westmorland New Tower for 1867–9	Major
4/93	Holker Holker Hall New wing Elizabethan style	Holker, N. Lancs, now Cumbria 1873	Major
4/94	Hornby Hornby Castle Additional work (ref: Ratter)	Hornby, N. Lancs 1879–82	Major
4/95	Hutton Roof St John New Church Perpendicular style	Westmorland, now Cumbria 1879–82	Major
4/96	Hoghton Tower Restoration	Hoghton, Nr Blackburn, N. Lancs post 1862	Major
4/97	Ince (Lower) St Mary New Church (Demolished 1974)	Lower Ince, S. Lancs 1887	Major
4/98	Kildwick St Andrew Restoration (also W. Window of N. Aisle 1859)	Kildwick, W. Yorks 1873	Major
4/99	Kirkby St Chad New Church Transitional/Romanesque style	Kirkby (Nr Liverpool) S. Lancs 1869–71	Major
4/100	Kirkby Malham St Michael Restoration	Kirkby Malham, W. Yorks 1879–81	Major
4/101	Knowsley	Knowsley, S. Lancs	Major

	St Mary Derby Chapel	1871–2	
4/102	Knutsford St Cross New Church Perpendicular style	Knutsford, Cheshire 1880–1	Major
4/103	Lancaster Lancaster Banking Co. New Bank (Church St)	Lancaster, Lancs 1870	Major
4/104	Lancaster Grammar School Extensions	Lancaster, Lancs 1877; 1881	Major
4/105	Lancaster i. Ripley Hospital Chapel ii. Other Buildings iii. Additions of W. Wing; Schools; Baths; Entrance Lodge	Lancaster, Lancs 1886–8 1885–6 1899?	Major
4/106	Lancaster Methodist Chapel New Chapel (Sulyard St)	Lancaster, Lancs 1873–4	Major
4/107	Lancaster Christ Church S. Aisle	Lancaster, Lancs 1889	Minor
4/108	Lancaster Christ Church W. Baptistry	Lancaster, Lancs 1871–2	Minor
4/109	Lancaster Militia Barracks Extension	Lancaster, Lancs 1871–2	Major
4/110	Lancaster The Knoll (private house for HJA)	Lancaster, Lancs 1879	Major
4/111	Lancaster St Peter i. Baptistry ii. Presbytery iii. Rose window in the Transept	Lancaster, Lancs c1895 1895–6 1888	Major
4/112	Lancaster Priory i. Work on chancel ii. Vestry and organ chamber	Lancaster, Lancs 1870 1882	Minor
4/113	Lancaster St Mary's School (Quay)	Lancaster, Lancs 1879–80	Major
4/114	Lancaster House in Regent Street for TD Smith	Lancaster, Lancs 1875	Major
4/115	Lancaster Royal Albert Rodget Infirmary	Lancaster, Lancs 1880–3	Major
4/116	Lancaster Royal Albert Winmarleigh Hall	Lancaster, Lancs 1888?	Major
4/117	Lancaster Town Hall extension	Lancaster, Lancs 1871	Major

	(Town clerk's office New Street)		
4/118	Lancaster Business premises for Mr W. Atkinson	Lancaster, Lancs no date	Major
4/119	Lancaster Gregson Institute	Lancaster, Lancs 1885–90	Major
4/120	Lancaster White Cross Mill Ornamental top to chimney	Lancaster, Lancs 1878	Minor
4/121	Lancaster/Skerton Ryelands House Extensions	Lancaster, Lancs 1883	Major
4/122	Langho St Leonard New Church Early English to Decorated style	Billington, N. Lancs 1879–80	Major
4/123	Leck St Peter New Church	Leck, N. Lancs 1878–9	Major
4/124	Leigh St Mary Restoration (except tower) Perpendicular (Brandwood)	Leigh, S. Lancs 1869–73	Major
4/125	Leyland St Andrew Restoration	Leyland, Lancs 1874	Major
4/126	Liverpool (Mossley) St Matthew & St James i. New Church ii. E. Window & Baptistry Late 13th Century style	Liverpool, S. Lancs 1870–5 1880	Major
4/127	Liverpool Mossley Hill Vicarage	Liverpool, S. Lancs 1873	Major
4/128	Llandovery Llandovery College Additional buildings	Llandovery, Carmathen no date	Major
4/129	Lytham St Cuthbert i. Chancel ii. N. Aisle	Lytham St Annes, Lancs 1872–3 1882	Major
4/130	Mansergh St Peter New Church Perpendicular style	Westmorland, now Cumbria 1880	Major
4/131	Melsonby St James the Great Rebuilt Nave and Restored church.	Melsonby, N. Yorks 1871–2	Major
4/132	Millom St George New Church Geometrical style	Millom, Cumberland Cumbria 1874–7	Major
4/133	Millom Station	Cumberland, now Cumbria 1874	Major
4/134	Morecambe	Morecambe, Lancs	Major

	St Laurence New Church Decorated style	1876–8	
4/135	Morecambe Promenade Railway Station	Morecambe, Lancs 1873	Major
4/136	Natland Sedgewick House New Mansion Perpendicular Gothic style	Natland, Westmorland now Cumbria 1868–9	Major
4/137	Newton Newton Hall New House	Newton, Whittington, N. Lancs 1880	Major
4/138	Ordsall St Clement New Church	Ordsall, Salford 1877–8	Major
4/139	Ormskirk St Peter & Paul Restoration	Ormskirk, Lancs. 1877–91	Major
4/140	Orton All Saints Restoration & enlargement	Westmorland, now Cumbria 1877–8	Major
4/141	Osmotherley St John Evangelist New Church	N. Lancs, now Cumbria 1874	Major
4/142	Oak Lea New House for Mr Schneider Demolished 1913 except Gate Lodge and Coach House (information from Michael Bottom- ley)	Barrow-in-Furness 1874	Major
4/143	Ouseburn (Great) St Mary the Virgin S. Chapel	Ouseburn, N. Yorks 1883	Major
4/144	Ouseburn (Little) Holy Trinity N. Aisle; Organ Chamber; E. Wall, alterations to window	Ouseburn, N. Yorks 1874–5	Major
4/145	Pilling St John the Baptist New Church	Pilling, Fylde, N. Lancs 1885–7	Major
4/146	Poulton-le-Fylde St Chad i. Apse & Chancel ii. Internal alterations (Stansfield feels that in addition to the internal alterations and renewal of Galleries in 1883, the Apse and Chancel are theirs).	Poulton-le-Fylde, Lancs 1860 1883	Major
4/147	Prestwick St Mary New chancel/Chapel; New roof; tower repair	Prestwick, S. Lancs 1872–4	Major
4/148	Ravenglass Station	Cumberland, near Cumbria no date	Major

4/149	Sandside Station	N. Lancs 1876	Major
4/150	St Annes on Sea St Anne i. New Church ii. Tower	St Annes, Fylde Coast, N. Lancs 1873–5 1887	Major
4/151	Scorton i. St Peter} New Church} Decorated style} ii. School} iii. Vicarage}	Scorton, N. Lancs 1878–9	Major
4/152	Seathwaite Holy Trinity New Church	Seathwaite, N. Lancs, now Cumbria 1874	Major
4/153	Seascale Station Weigh House and Water Tower?	Cumberland, now Cumbria 1877	Minor
4/154	Sedbergh i. School House ii. Sedgewick House	Sedbergh, W. Yorks 1878 1879	Major
4/155	Sedbergh St Andrew Restoration	Sedbergh, W. Yorks 1886	Major
4/156	Shrewsbury St Mary the Virgin N. vestry	Shrewsbury, Shropshire 1884	Minor
4/157	St Johns Chapel Town Hall	St Johns Chapel, C. Durham 1868	Major
4/158	Skipton Ermystead Grammar School	Skipton, W. Yorks 1872–4	Major
4/159	St Bees School House	St Bees, Cumberland, now Cumbria 1885	Major
4/160	Stockton Heath St Thomas New Church Decorated style (1300)	Stockton Heath, Warrington, Lancs 1868–9	Major
4/161	Tatham St Thomas Restoration	Tatham, N. Lancs 1885–7	Major
4/162	Tatham Fells The Good Shepherd Church Rebuilt Late Perpendicular style	Tatham, N. Lancs 1888–9	Major
4/163	Thornton-in-Lonsdale St Oswald Rebuilt Perpendicular style	Thornton-in-Lonsdale, W. Yorks 1869–70	Major
4/164	Thorpe Bassett All Saints Restoration	Thorpe Bassett, E. Yorks 1879–80	Major
4/165	Torver St Luke New Church Norman style	N. Lancs, now Cumbria 1884	Major
4/166	Tunstall	Tunstall, N. Lancs	Major

	Thurland Castle Semi Elizabethan/ Semi Gothic style	1879–88	
4/167	Ulverston i. Station ii. Stables	N. Lancs, now Cumbria 1872–4 1875	Major
4/168	Ulverston St Mary Work in Chancel; replaced E. window	N. Lancs, now Cumbria 1879–82	Major
4/169	Underley Additions to the hall new wing and tower	Kirkby Lonsdale, Westmorland now Cumbria 1873	Major
4/170	Walmsley Christ Church additions	Turton, Nr Bolton, S. Lancs. no date	
4/171	Walton St Mary New Church	Cumberland, Cumbria 1869–70	Major
4/172	Walton (Higher Walton) St John the Evangelist New Church Decorated style	Higher Walton, Cheshire 1882–5	Major
4/173	Walton (Higher Walton) Walton Hall Additions/alterations	Cheshire 1870	Major
4/174	Walton-le-Dale Higher Walton All Saints New Steeple 13th Century style	Walton-le-Dale, Lancashire 1871	Major
4/175	Walton-le-Dale All Saints School	Walton-le-Dale, Lancashire 1884	Major
4/176	Westleigh St Peter New Church Decorated style	Leigh, Lancs 1880–1	Major
4/177	Whitehaven Colliery Schools	Cumberland, now Cumbria 1876	Major
4/178	Whittington St Michael Restoration	Whittington, Lancs 1875	Major
4/179	Whittington i. Additions/alterations to Whittington Hall inc. Billiard Room ii. Lodge iii. House Farm Dairy 1885	Whittington, Lancs 1870–90 1890 1885	Major
4/180	Wilmington St Mary and St Peter New Church	Wilmington, Sussex 1883	Major
4/181	Winmarleigh St Luke New Church N. Aisle Enlarged	N. Lancs 1876–7 1877 1887	Major
4/182	Winmarleigh Hall/Stables	N. Lancs 1871	Major

	Jacobean style		
4/183	Winmarleigh School and School house	N. Lancs 1870	Major
4/184	Windermere Chapel Ridding House	Westmorland, now Cumbria no date	Major
4/185	Windermere St Mary additions	Westmorland, now Cumbria 1881–2	Major
4/186	Winwick St Oswald Restoration and rebuilt spire	S. Lancs 1869	Major
4/187	Witherslack Witherslack Hall	Witherslack, N. Lancs, now Cumbria 1874	Major
4/188	Wolverhampton (Penn) Additions to St Bartholomew Style of 1300	Staffs. 1871–2	Major
4/189	Wrea Green St Nicholas Tower and Spire	Wrea Green, N. Lancs 1884	Major
4/190	Wray Holy Trinity New Chancel	Wray, N. Lancs 1879	Major
4/191	Yarm St Mary Magdalene Restoration & enlargement	Yarm, N. Yorks 1878	Major
4/192	Yealand Conyers Leighton Hall West Wing	N. Lancs 1870	Major

The Buildings of Paley, Austin and Paley, 1886–95

5/01	Abberley Abberley Hall Chapel	Hereford & Worcester 1889	Major
5/02	Accrington St Peter's Vicarage	Accrington, Lancs 1889	Major
5/03	Barbon St Bartholemew New Church Perpendicular style	Westmorland, Cumbria 1892–3	Major
5/04	Barrow-in-Furness Additions to house in St George's Square	N. Lancs/Cumbria 1890	Minor
5/05	Birkdale St John New Church Enlarged	Southport, S. Lancs 1889–90 1903–9	Major
5/06	Blackburn i. St Silas New Church Decorated style ii. Tower	Blackburn, Lancs 1894–8 1913–4	Major
5/07	Borwick (Priest Hutton) St Mary New Church	Lancs 1894–6	Major
5/08	Bootle	Cumberland, Cumbria	Minor

	Chancel fittings and pulpit	1890	
5/09	Bowness-on-Solway St Michael N. transept	Cumberland now Cumbria 1891	Major
5/10	Bury Parish Church Chancel seats	Bury, Lancs 1894	Minor
5/11	Cheetham St John the Evangelist Restoration	Manchester 1895	Major
5/12	Cloughfold St John New Church Perpendicular style	Rawtenstall, Lancs 1890	Major
5/13	Colne St Bartholomew Interior Restoration (removed N. aisle replaced by double aisle. P. Milner)	Colne, N. Lancs 1889–90	Major
5/14	Colton Rusland Holy Trinity Restoration	Rusland, N. Lancs now Cumbria 1890	Major
5/15	Coventry St Michael Campanile/Bell Tower Not built	Coventry, Warwickshire 1888, 1891	Major
5/16	Crawshawbooth St John the Evangelist New Church Perpendicular style	Rawtenstall, Lancs 1890–2	Major
5/17	Dent St Andrew Restoration	W. Yorks 1889–90	Major
5/18	Farnworth St Luke Restoration	Widnes, S. Lancs 1892–5	Major
5/19	Fence Hoarstones additions to house	Higham, Lancs. 1894	Major
5/20	Field Broughton St Peter New Church Perpendicular style	N. Lancs, now Cumbria 1893–4	Major
5/21	Giggleswick Giggleswick School Classroom; Gym; Covered playground	Giggleswick, Settle N. Yorks 1886	Major
5/22	Halton Manor House Additions	Halton, N. Lancs 1899	Minor
5/23	Heaviley St George New Church	Stockport, Cheshire 1893–7	Major
5/24	Heaviley Vicarage	Stockport, Cheshire 1897	Major
5/25	Heaviley Schools	Stockport, Cheshire 1904?	Major
5/26	Highfield	Wigan, S. Lancs	Major

	St Matthew New Church Early English style Enlarged Reredos	1892–4 1910 1917	
5/27	Horsham Christ's Hospital School (Not built)	Horsham, Sussex 1893	Major
5/28	Hornby Hornby Castle	Hornby, N. Lancs 1889	Major
5/29	Hornby St Margaret New Nave	Hornby, N. Lancs 1888–9	Major
5/30	Ince in Makerfield St Mary New Church	Ince in Makerfield, S. Lancs 1887	Major
5/31	Lancaster St Mary Restoration of E. Window	Lancaster, Lancs 1892	Minor
5/32	Lancaster Royal Infirmary	Lancaster, Lancs 1893–6	Major
5/33	Lancaster Storey Institute	Lancaster, Lancs 1887–91	Major
5/34	Lancaster St George Mission Church Marsh	Lancaster, Lancs 1898	Major
5/35	Lancaster Mission Church Dale Street	Lancaster, Lancs 1891	Major
5/36	Lancaster Alteration to St Mary National School	Lancaster, Lancs 1896	Major
5/37	Preston Patrick St Gregory Chancel replaced	Westmorland, Cumbria 1892	Major
5/38	Prestwich St Mary Additions/restoration	Prestwich, S. Lancs 1888–9	Major
5/39	Rossall Rossall School W. Range	Rossall, Fleetwood, Lancs 1885	Major
5/40	Scarborough St James New Church	N. Yorks 1885	Major
5/41	Scotforth St Paul W. End/transepts	Scotforth, Lancaster 1892	Major
5/42	Sedbergh Sedbergh School Chapel	W. Yorks 1897	Major
5/43	Sutton All Saints New Church	St Helens, S. Lancs 1891–3	Major
5/44	Tunstall Thurland Castle additional work	N. Lancs 1888	Major
5/45	Unsworth	Bury, S. Lancs	Major

	St George additions	no date	
5/46	Warton St Oswald Restoration	Warton, N. Lancs 1892	Major
5/47	Waterloo Christ Church New Church Perpendicular style	Liverpool 1891–9	Major
5/48	Wesham Christ Church Nave only	Kirkham, Fylde, Lancs 1893–4	Major
5/49	Witherslack St Paul Oak Reredos	Westmorland, now Cumbria 1889	Minor
5/50	Worsthorne St John the Evangelist Restoration/chancel/ tower	Burnley, Lancs 1894	Major
5/51	Wray Holy Trinity New Nave roof and alterations to W. Elevation	Wray, N. Lancs 1889	Major

The Works of Austin and Paley, 1895–Jan. 1914

6/01	Acton St Mary Restoration only	Acton, Cheshire 1897–8	Major
6/02	Alsager St Mary Magdalene New Church Decorated style	Alsager, Cheshire 1894–8	Major
6/03	Altrincham St George 'some rebuilding'/ restoration	Altrincham, Cheshire 1896–7	Major
6/04	Altrincham St Alban New Church	Altrincham, Cheshire 1900	Major
6/05	Arkholme Church Restoration	Arkholme, N. Lancs 1897(?)	Major
6/06	Arnside St James Extended and altered	Westmorland, now Cumbria 1912–4	Major
6/07	Ashton on Ribble St Michael and All Angels i. New Church Perpendicular style ii. Additions	Preston, Lancs 1906–8 1915	Major
6/08	Atherton St Anne New Church Decorated style	Atherton, S. Lancs 1898–1901	Major
6/09	Balderstone St Leonard Added tower/spire	Nr Mellor, N. Lancs 1906–7	Major

6/10	Balterley New Church	Balterley, Staffs 1901	Major
6/11	Barnacre All Saints New Church	Barnacre, N. Lancs 1905	Major
6/12	Barrow-in-Furness North Lonsdale Hospital: Laundry New Medical Wing New Operating Rooms	N. Lancs, now Cumbria 1896 1899 1903	Major
6/13	Bolton Halliwell St Margaret New Church Free Decorated Tracery	Bolton, Lancs 1903	Major
6/14	Bolton-by-Bowland Additions to school	W. Yorks 1906	Major
6/15	Bootle Village Cross	Bootle, Cumberland now Cumbria 1897	Minor
6/16	Brathay Holy Trinity Additions to.	Nr Ambleside, Westmorland, now Cumbria 1905	Major
6/17	Bretherton St John the Baptist Chancel added; renovation	Bretherton, N. Lancs 1909	Major
6/18	Broughton St John the Baptist New Chancel	Nr. Preston, N. Lancs 1905–6	Major
6/19	Broughton-in-Furness St Mary Magdalene New S. W. Tower	N. Lancs, now Cumbria 1900	Major
6/20	Broughton-in-Furness Foxfield Station Additions	N. Lancs, now Cumbria 1900	Major
6/21	Casterton Holy Trinity New Reredos	Westmorland, now Cumbria 1897	Minor
6/22	Claughton St Chad Restoration	Nr Hornby, N. Lancs 1904	Major
6/23	Cockerham St Michael Rebuilt Perpendicular style	N. Lancs 1910	Major
6/24	Constable Lee St Paul New Church	Nr Rawtenstall, Lancs 1899–1903	Major
6/25	Dolphinholme St Mark New Church	Dolphinholme, N. Lancs 1897–99	Major
6/26	Ellel St John New Church	Ellel, Galgate N. Lancs 1906–7	Major
6/27	Flookburgh St John the Baptist New Church	Flookburgh, N. Lancs now Cumbria 1897–1900	Major

	Romanesque style		
6/28	Great Harwood St John New Church	Gt Harwood, N. Lancs 1911–2	Major
6/29	Grasmere Michaels Fold Extension to house for Misses Paley	Cumberland, now Cumbria 1911	Major
6/30	Grindleton St Ambrose Rebuilt	Nr Clitheroe, N. Lancs 1897–8	Major
6/31	Hampson Green Hampson House extended	Forton, N. Lancs c1900	Major
6/32	Hertford All Saints New Church Perpendicular style	Hertford, Herts 1895–1905	Major
6/33	Hertford House for Mr Swordlis	Hertford, Herts no date	Major
6/34	High Bentham St Margaret Chancel	High Bentham, W. Yorks 1902	Major
6/35	Kendal St George Chancel added	Kendal, Westmorland now Cumbria 1907–11	Major
6/36	Kirkby Lonsdale 'Greenclose' House and surgery	Westmorland, now Cumbria c1900	Major
6/37	Kirkby Lonsdale Market Cross Alterations	Westmorland, now Cumbria 1905	Minor
6/38	Kildwick St Andrew Chancel and Nave Restored	Kildwick, W. Yorks 1901–3	Major
6/39	Knott End St Oswald New Church	Preesall, N. Lancs 1896–8	Major
6/40	Lancaster Lancaster and Skerton Equitable Industrial Coopera- tive Society, (in addition they designed the branch shops and the Warehouse Building in Bulk Street)	Lancaster, Lancs Head Office and shop in New Street 1901	
6/41	Lancaster 96 Church Street Converted to Church Hall for the Priory	Lancaster, Lancs 1910	Major
6/42	Lancaster Storey Institute Additions	Lancaster, Lancs 1903	Major
6/43	Lancaster Royal Albert New South Wing (Ashton Wing)	Lancaster, Lancs 1898–1901	Major
6/44	Lancaster Nazareth House New Orphanage	Lancaster, Lancs 1901–2	Major

6/45	Lancaster Covell Cross	Lancaster, Lancs 1902–3	Minor
6/46	Lancaster Ripley (Hospital) Orphanage Additions: Sanatorium Gymnasium Classrooms	Lancaster, Lancs 1898 1897 1897	Major
6/47	Lancaster St Mary Additions: Porch Hatch Memorial Chapel Restoration (inc. Nave Roof; Chancel floor)	Lancaster, Lancs 1902 1902 1903–4 1911–2	Major
6/48	Lancaster Garage for Mr Atkinson	Lancaster, Lancs 1904	Major
6/49	Lancaster Alexandra Hotel	Lancaster, Lancs 1902	Major
6/50	Lancaster St Peter's Boys School New School	Lancaster, Lancs 1897	Major
6/51	Leck St Peter Rebuilt after a fire	Leck, N. Lancs 1915	Major
6/52	Leeds Leeds Grammar School Extensions	Leeds, W. Yorks 1904–5	Major
6/53	Leigh St Mary New Vestry	Leigh, Lancs 1910	Major
6/54	Liverpool Anglican Cathedral Commission entry (not built)	Liverpool, Lancs 1902–3	Major
6/55	Mellor St Mary Restoration	Mellor, Nr Blackburn, Lancs 1899	Major
6/56	Middleton St Michael and All Angels New Church	Middleton, S. Lancs 1902	Major
6/57	Morecambe St Barnabas New Church Perpendicular style	Morecambe, Lancs 1898–1910	Major
6/58	Morecambe St John (Sandylands) New Church	Morecambe, Lancs 1899–1901	Major
6/59	Myerscough Myerscough Hall Alterations	Myerscough, N. Lancs no date	Major
6/60	Natland St Mark New Church Perpendicular style	Natland, Westmorland, now Cumbria 1909–10	Major
6/61	Newton Heath St Wilfrid New Church	Newton Heath, Manchester 1908–10	Major

6/62	Newton Heath Rectory for St Wilfrid	Newton Heath, 1914	Major
6/63	Newland Newland Hall Additions: Kitchen Billiard Room Entrance Hall	Newland, Nr Galgate N. Lancs 1908 1913 1913	Major
6/64	Overton St Helen Restoration	Overton, N. Lancs 1909	Major
6/65	Over Kellet Church Restoration	Over Kellet, N. Lancs 1909	Major
6/66	Pudsey (Waterloo) St James New Church	Pudsey, W. Yorks 1914	Major
6/67	Redmarshall St Cuthbert New Church	Redmarshall, Co. Durham 1904	Major
6/68	Ribbleton St Mary Magdalene Additions	Farringdon, Ribbleton, Preston, N. Lancs c1901	Major
6/69	Rossall Rossall School New Chapel St John the Baptist	Rossall, Fleetwood Lancs 1902	Major
6/70	Rossall Rossall School Additions: School Room Dining Room	Rossall, Fleetwood Lancs 1897 no date	Major
6/71	Rossall Mission Church Vestry	Rossall, Fleetwood Lancs 1888–9	Minor
6/72	St Bees St Bees School: Chapel} Headmasters House} Labs} Library}	Cumberland, now Cumbria 1907–10	Major
6/73	Sedbergh Sedbergh School Powell Hall	Sedbergh, W. Yorks 1906	Major
6/74	Skelmersdale St Paul New Church Perpendicular style	Skelmersdale, N. Lancs 1903–6	Major
6/75	Slyne New Church Decorated/Free Perpendicular style	Slyne,Nr Lancaster, Lancs 1900	Major
6/76	Skipton Parish Church New Vestries; seating, Bell ringers loft, Restoration/additions inc. removal of Galleries	Skipton, W. Yorks 1909	Major
6/77	Standish St Wilfred	Standish, Nr Parbold, S. Lancs	Major

	East Vestries Additions	1913–4	
6/78	Starbeck St Andrew New Church	Starbeck, Harrogate, N. Yorks 1909–10	Major
6/79	Starbeck Church Hall	Starbeck, Harrogate N. Yorks 1919	Major
6/80	St Annes St Thomas New Church Decorated/Perpendicular style	St Annes, Fylde, Lancs 1895–1905	Major
6/81	Sunderland Point Mission Church	Overton, N. Lancs 1894	Major
6/82	Thornbury St Margaret New Church	Thornbury, Bradford W. Yorks 1911–2	Major
6/83	Tunstall St John the Baptist Restoration	Tunstall, N. Lancs 1907	Major
6/84	Ulverston St Mary Work on Chancel; windows; new transept	N. Lancs, now Cumbria 1905	Minor
6/85	Walney Island St Mary the Virgin New Church (rebuild)	Barrow-in-Furness, Lancs, now Cumbria 1907–8	Major
6/86	Whicham St Mary Restoration	Nr Millom, Cumberland now Cumbria 1902	Major
6/87	Widnes St Mary New Church Perpendicular style	Widnes, S. Lancs 1908–10	Major
6/88	Woodplumpton St Anne Additions/Restoration	Nr Preston, N. Lancs 1899–1900	Major
6/89	Woodplumpton Vicarage Enlarged	Nr Preston, N. Lancs 1908	Minor
6/90	Worksop St Anne New Church Perpendicular style	Nottinghamshire 1910–12	Major
6/91	Worsthorne St John the Evangelist New Tower	Nr Burnley, Lancs 1903	Major

The Works of Austin, Paley and Austin – January 1914-February 1915

7/01	Basford St Mark New Church	Newcastle U. Lyme, Staffs 1914–5	Major
7/02	Thornton Christ Church Chapel Chancel only	Thornton, Cleveleys Blackpool 1914	Major
7/03	Hertford	Herts	Minor

	St George Reredos	1914	
7/04	Blawith St John the Baptist Restoration	N. Lancs, now Cumbria 1914	Major

The Works of Austin and Paley 1916–1944, i.e. The Work of H. A. Paley

8/01	Abram St John New Church	Abram, S. Lancs 1935–7	Major
8/02	Acton St Mary Tower Repairs	Nantwich, Cheshire 1925	Major
8/03	Alsager St Mary Completion of N. Porch and Aisles	Alsager, Cheshire 1936–7	Major
8/04	Aldingham St Cuthbert Repairs to windows/ roughcast walls	N. Lancs, now Cumbria 1931	Minor
8/05	Atherton St John the Baptist Vestry	S. Lancs 1938	Minor
8/06	Ashton in Makerfield New Vestry	S. Lancs 1929–30	Minor
8/07	Ashton on Ribble St Michael Organ floor; walls	Nr Preston, Lancs 1934+	Minor
8/08	Barthomley St Bertoline Restoration and New Chancel	Cheshire 1925–6	Major
8/09	Basford St Mark New Vestry	Newcastle U. Lyme, Staffs 1928–9	Minor
8/10	Becconsall All Saints: New Church Tower	Hesketh, N. Lancs 1923–6 1935–6	Major
8/11	Bilsborrow St Hilda New Church	Bilsborrow, N. Lancs 1926–7	Major
8/12	Bilsborrow Vicarage	Bilsborrow, N. Lancs 1930+	Major
8/13	Blawith St John the Baptist Renovation of N. W. wall/ buttresses	N. Lancs now Cumbria 1926+	Major
8/14	Bolton St Thomas Halliwell New Vestry	Halliwell, Bolton, Lancs 1931–2	Minor
8/15	Bolton St Margaret Vestry and offices	Bolton, Lancs 1939	Minor
8/16	Bolton-le-Sands Proposed Organ chamber	N. Lancs 1940	Minor

	at St Michaels Church		
8/17	Walney Island St Mary W. End and Vestry	Barrow-in-Furness, Cumbria 1930–1	Major
8/18	Barton on Irwell School	S. Lancs no date	Major
8/19	Blackpool St Stephen on the Cliffs New Church	Fylde, N. Lancs 1924–6	Major
8/20	Blackpool St Thomas New Church	Fylde, N. Lancs 1929–32	Major
8/21	Burnley St Matthew Rebuilt	Lancs. 1929–31	Major
8/22	Carnforth New HQ for Kings Own	N. Lancs 1929+	Major
8/23	Casterton Casterton School Additional classrooms	Westmorland, now Cumbria 1929–30	Major
8/24	Caton War Memorial	Caton, N. Lancs 1922	Minor
8/25	Caton Extensions to Victoria Institute	Caton, N. Lancs 1928	Minor
8/26	Coventry St Barnabas New Church	Warwickshire 1932–4	Major
8/27	Crawshawbooth St John Memorial Chapel	Rawtenstall, Lancs 1931	Minor
8/28	Crewe Green St Michael Proposed alterations	Cheshire 1939+	Minor
8/29	Earlsdon, St Barbara New Church (Memorial Chapel to Sir Alfred Herbert 1931)	Coventry, Warwickshire 1930–1	Major
8/30	Eaton War (?) Memorial	Tarporley, Cheshire 1936+	Minor
8/31	Feniscowles Immanuel Restoration	Blackburn, Lancs 1931–2	Major
8/32	Giggleswick Giggleswick School: Sanatorium Chemistry Lab	W./N. Yorks 1929–40 1930+	Major
8/33	Glasson Christ Church New Chancel and Vestry	Glasson, Nr Lancaster Lancs 1931–2	Major
8/34	Glasson Vault/Monument and Stone slab to Dalton family	Glasson, Nr Lancaster 1932 1939–40	Minor
8/35	Grange-over-Sands St Paul New Chancel and additions	Lancs, now Cumbria 1932–3	Major
8/36	Kendal Heaves House	Kendal, Westmorland Cumbria 1932	Minor

	Alterations for Lady Ashton		
8/37	Keswick Keswick High School	Cumberland now Cumbria no date	no idea of scale
8/38	Lancaster Christ Church War Memorial	Lancaster, Lancs 1920	Minor
8/39	Lancaster Royal Grammar School Dormitory Block	Lancaster, Lancs 1933	Minor
8/40	Lancaster Penny's Hospital Restoration	Lancaster, Lancs 1929	Major
8/41	Lancaster Business Premises for SB Wilding Damside St	Lancaster, Lancs 1937	Major
8/42	Lancaster St Peter's Cathedral Repairs	Lancaster, Lancs 1928, 1931–2, 1939, 1944	Minor
8/43	Lancaster St Peter's Senior School Alterations	Lancaster, Lancs 1930–1	Minor
8/44	Lancaster Royal Lancaster Infirmary Nurses Home	Lancaster, Lancs 1929–32, 1935	Major
8/45	Lancaster Royal Infirmary Alterations and additions Kitchen; Maternity/Children's Ward; Staff Dining Room; X Ray Dept	Lancaster, Lancs 1929–40	Major
8/46	Lancaster New Bedroom Wing Nurses Home, Regent St	Lancaster, Lancs 1935	Major
8/47	Lancaster Christ Church School Additions/Alterations	Lancaster, Lancs 1928–9	Major
8/48	Lancaster Priory Hall	Lancaster, Lancs 1936–9	Major
8/49	Lathom St James New Vestries	Lancs 1939	Minor
8/50	Leeds Leeds Grammar School: Science Labs Memorial Swimming Pool	W. Yorks 1925–6 1928–9	Major
8/51	Long Whatton Church Memorial Baptistry	Leicestershire 1931	Minor
8/52	Lytham St Cuthbert New Memorial Morning Chapel	Lytham, Fylde N. Lancs 1931+	Major
8/53	Melling Church Gate House Alterations	Nr Lancaster, N. Lancs 1930	Minor
8/54	Middleton St Michael and All Angels	Middleton, Lancs 1929–30	Major

	New Tower		
8/55	Morecambe St Christopher, Bare New Church	Morecambe, Lancs 1932–4	Major
8/56	Newton-le-Willows Church Vestries; Porch; Offices	Lancs 1932+	Minor
8/57	Orrell St Luke New Church Completed	Wigan, Lancs 1927–8 1936–8	Major
8/58	Orrell Vicarage	Wigan, Lancs 1931–2	Major
8/59	Pennington New Chancel; Porch; restoration of Tower	N. Lancs, now Cumbria 1924–6	Major
8/60	Penrith Burbank House Additions/alterations	Cumberland, now Cumbria 1925+	Minor
8/61	Pilling War Memorial	N. Lancs 1920	Minor
8/62	Preston New Vicarage (not built)	Preston, N. Lancs 1920s	Major
8/63	Preston St Matthew Completion of Chancel, Chapel and Vestries	Preston, N. Lancs 1933	Major
8/64	Preston Christ Church Chapel of Remembrance	Preston, N. Lancs 1937+	Major
8/65	Preston Fulwood Parish Church Renovation and Repairs	Preston, N. Lancs 1934–5	Major
8/66	Preston St John Proposed Vergers House	Preston, N. Lancs 1939	Major
8/67	Ribbleton St Mary Magdalene New Chancel, Chapel, Aisles and Vestries	Preston, Lancs 1938–41	Major
8/68	Ribby with Wrea St Nicholas Work on Parsonage House and Cottage	N. Lancs 1932–3	Minor
8/69	Ribby with Wrea St Nicholas New Choir floor and seats	N. Lancs 1931–2	Minor
8/70	Sandbach St Mary New Vestry and Porch	Cheshire 1929–30	Minor
8/71	Scotforth Scotforth School Staffroom/alterations	Lancaster, Lancs 1938	Minor
8/72	Scotforth St Paul Redecoration and new doorway	Lancaster, Lancs 1932+	Minor
8/73	Sedbergh	W. Yorks	Major

	Wide range of additions inc. Powell Hall	1922–1938	
	Memorial Cloister	1922	
	Sanatorium	1932	
8/74	Skerton St Luke's Junior School New School	Skerton, Lancaster 1928–9	Major
8/75	Singleton St Anne New Vestry	Singleton, N. Lancs 1938	Minor
8/76	St Annes St Anne New Memorial Vestry Additions	Lytham St Annes, Fylde, N. Lancs 1930–1 1919	Minor
8/77	Slaidburn Proposed Central School	W. Yorks (now Lancs) 1939+	Major
8/78	Slyne with Hest Beaumont Cote Hall Additions and 2 cottages	Nr Lancaster, Lancs 1927	Major
8/79	Standish Church Gatehouse and War Memorial	Wigan, Lancs 1926	Minor
8/80	Skipton Parish Church New N. Transept roof repairs	W. Yorks 1925	Minor
8/81	Thornton le Fylde Christ Church New Tower and Nave	Fylde, N. Lancs 1936+	Major
8/82	Thornton in Lonsdale Repair after fire	W. Yorks 1934–6	Major
8/83	Tunstall Alterations to Tunstall House	N. Lancs 1936	Minor
8/84	Ulverston St Mary S. Chancel Aisle converted to War Memorial Chapel	N. Lancs now Cumbria 1923	Minor
8/85	Wennington 'Cravens' alterations to a house	N. Lancs 1932	Minor
8/86	Wesham Christ Church Enlarged and completed	Kirkham, Lancs 1927–8	Major
8/87	Whelley St Stephen: Begun Completed	Whelley, Wigan S. Lancs 1927–30 1937–8	Major
8/88	Winwick St Oswald: Gerrard Chapel Restored Tower Restored	S. Lancs 1929 1931	Major
8/89	Worksop St Anne's Vicarage	Notts 1929	Major
8/90	Worksop St Anne Memorial to Sir John Robinson	Notts 1931	Minor

Appendix B
Paley and Austin and the Furness Railway by Mr Phillip Grosse

Paley and Austin did work for the Furness Railway from the early 1860s.

The following buildings are known to have been designed by Paley and Austin through existing archival plans.

1862	Barrow in Furness 'Strand' station buildings
1862	Coniston Station
1862	St George's Square Railway Offices FR headquarters
1865	Grange over Sands station buildings
1865	Cark in Cartmel station waiting shelter (demolished)
1872–78	Ulverston (cost £10,000)
1874	Millom Station
1875	Kirby in Furness station buildings (demolished)
1876	Sandside (demolished)
1877	Foxfield (demolished)
1880	Barrow Central (destroyed 1942) cost £15,000
1883	Carnforth (Furness and Midland) extension to station
1883	Ulverston Canal-Hydraulic Engine House (demolished)
1883	Conishead Priory station building

Other work likely to have been undertaken

1869	Greenodd, Haverthwaite and Windermere (Lakeside) station buildings
1885	Whitehaven Bransty station buildings
1885	Bootle, Drigg, Seascale, Ravenglass and Sellafield station buildings

Appendix C
The Construction of the Distribution Maps
by Stewart Mousir-Harrison

The procedure to create the maps of the distribution of the works of the eight Lancaster architectural practices typified by Paley and Austin comprised a number of steps.

1) Digitisation of Coastline

The outline for the maps was digitised from the Ordnance Survey 1 : 2,000,000 scale key map for the Seventh Series of One Inch to One Mile (1 : 63,360) sheets. This gave a suitable base map, which was reproduced at a scale of approximately 1 : 185,185 on the original A4 printed output. The outline encompasses England as far south east as Cambridge and north east as Alnwick, Scotland south of Ayr and Wales north of Cardigan, with the majority of the works being carried out in Lancashire.

2) Database Construction

To allow the easy storage and retrieval of the information a database was created recording the architect/originator of the design, the primary location (nearest town or part of country), the dates of the start and finishing of the work, the degree of work undertaken and some further codes for data sorting that have not been used to date. For the purposes of map creation, however, the most important feature is the Ordnance Survey Grid Reference, taken from the OS Gazetteer of Great Britain (1969) which lists all features on the Quarter Inch (Fifth Series) Maps, to within a kilometre. Such a resolution is perfectly satisfactory given the final scale of the maps.

A sample record:

Originator	*Paley & Austin*	*Date(s): 1878*
		Date(f): 1897
Location 1:	Atherton	OS Ref: 367, 403
Location 2:	S. Lancs	Class: Major
Type 1:	New Church (S. John Baptist)	Tr 1: D
Type 2:	New Tower (S. John Baptist)	Tr 2: D
Type 3:	Extension (S. John Baptist)	Tr 3: D

3) Map Construction

The final maps were created in a simple raster-based Geographic Information System (GIS) on an IBM-compatible PC with the output directed to a standard inkjet printer. The relevant portions of the database were accessed by the GIS and combined with the digitised outline maps and a set of commands to provide the legend and text to produce the final set of maps. Only seven locations of work, actual or intended, falling outside the area digitised for the outline were not mapped.

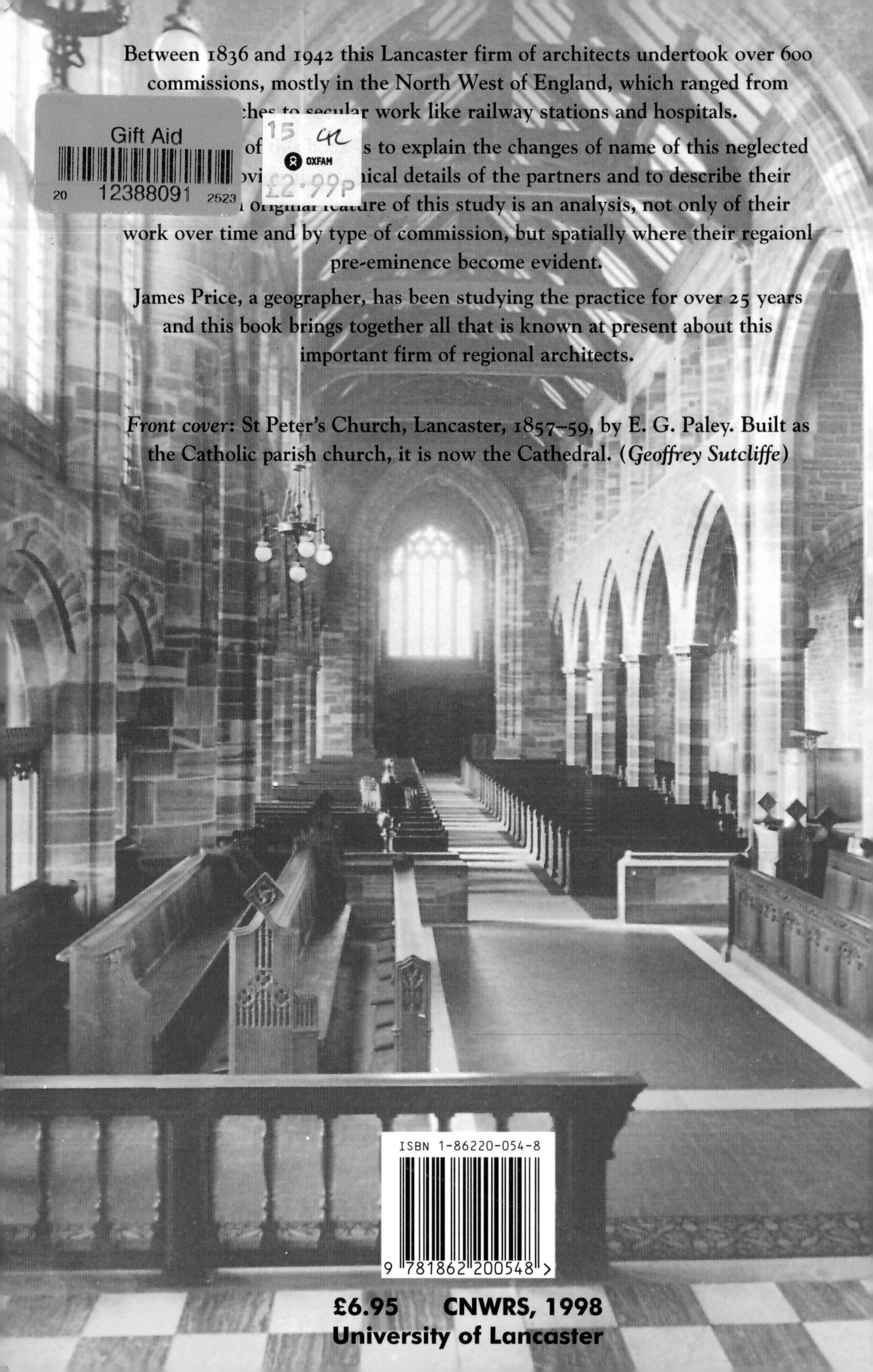

Between 1836 and 1942 this Lancaster firm of architects undertook over 600 commissions, mostly in the North West of England, which ranged from ches to secular work like railway stations and hospitals.

of s to explain the changes of name of this neglected vi ical details of the partners and to describe their original feature of this study is an analysis, not only of their work over time and by type of commission, but spatially where their regaionl pre-eminence become evident.

James Price, a geographer, has been studying the practice for over 25 years and this book brings together all that is known at present about this important firm of regional architects.

Front cover: St Peter's Church, Lancaster, 1857–59, by E. G. Paley. Built as the Catholic parish church, it is now the Cathedral. (*Geoffrey Sutcliffe*)

ISBN 1-86220-054-8
9 781862 200548 >

£6.95 CNWRS, 1998
University of Lancaster